# SAIPAN 1944

# SAIPAN 1944
## THE MOST DECISIVE BATTLE OF THE PACIFIC WAR

JOHN GREHAN & ALEXANDER NICOLL

Frontline Books

# SAIPAN 1944
## The Most Decisive Battle of the Pacific War

First published in Great Britain in 2021 by Frontline Books,
an imprint of Pen & Sword Books Ltd,
Yorkshire – Philadelphia

Copyright © John Grehan and Alexander Nicoll
ISBN: 978-1-52675-830-9

Typeset in 9.5/12.5 Avenir by Dave Cassan.
Printed and bound by CPI Group (UK) Ltd, Croydon, CR0 4YY

Pen & Sword Books Ltd incorporates the imprints of Air World Books, Pen & Sword Archaeology, Atlas, Aviation, Battleground, Discovery, Family History, History, Maritime, Military, Naval, Politics, Social History, Transport, True Crime, Claymore Press, Frontline Books, Praetorian Press, Seaforth Publishing and White Owl.

For a complete list of Pen & Sword titles please contact:

**PEN & SWORD BOOKS LTD**
47 Church Street, Barnsley, South Yorkshire, S70 2AS, UK.
E-mail: enquiries@pen-and-sword.co.uk
Website: www.pen-and-sword.co.uk

Or

**PEN AND SWORD BOOKS,**
1950 Lawrence Road, Havertown, PA 19083, USA
E-mail: Uspen-and-sword@casematepublishers.com
Website: www.penandswordbooks.com

# CONTENTS

# ACKNOWLEDGEMENTS

The authors and publisher would like to extend their grateful thanks, in no particular order, to the following individuals and organisations for their assistance with the images used in this publication: Robert Mitchell, James Luto, Historic Military Press, US Naval History and Heritage Command, US National Museum of Naval Aviation, National Archives and Records Administration, National Museum of the US Air Force, United States Air Force, US Navy, US Library of Congress, United States Marine Corps, USMC Archives, US Army, and the US War Department.

# OPERATION FORAGER

By 1943, the nature of the war in the Pacific was changing. No longer were the Japanese advancing over vast swathes of sea and land to extend the Imperial Empire. Now it was the turn of the United States and its Allies.

The rapid capture of the Gilbert and Marshall Islands and Tarawa from late 1943 and early 1944 had seen American forces isolating and destroying the Japanese occupying forces. While these victories, and the speed of the Allied advance through the Pacific, surprised the Japanese, they did little to change the strategic situation in the region. Tokyo and the main Japanese island of Honshu were still far beyond the reach of USAAF bombers on any of the recently captured territories.

There was no likelihood of an end to the war until the Japanese homeland and its people were directly threatened and, after the tenacious resistance shown by their defence of captured territory – particularly at 'Bloody Tarawa' – the prospect of having to fight all the way to Tokyo was an unwelcome one. But coming off the production lines at Boeing was the new B-29 Superfortress which had an operational range in excess of 2,800 miles – and sitting just 1,200 miles from Tokyo were the Japanese-held Mariana Islands. It was to the largest of these islands, namely Saipan, Guam and Tinian, that the US Joint Chiefs turned their attention in the spring of 1944.

Admiral Ernest J. King, the American Chief of Naval Operations, had long argued that the Marianas were the strategic key to the entire western Pacific. Land-based fighter and bomber aircraft on these islands controlled the sea lanes to Japan and protected the home islands, so their capture would sever Japan's communications with the rest of its shrinking empire.

Not everyone agreed with him, especially General Douglas MacArthur, Commander-in-Chief Southwest Pacific Area, who was fixated upon returning to the Philippines, as he had promised when he was evacuated from there on 11 March 1942. MacArthur demanded that all effort should be focussed on re-conquering the Philippines and believed that any offensive against the central Pacific islands should be dropped. He saw the Philippines as being the base from which the invasion of Japan could be launched and that all the American effort should therefore be concentrated on that goal. But the B-29 had been developed expressly for the purpose of bombing Japan, and at a cost of $2.04 billion was by far the most expensive weapons system of the Second World War. Consequently, there was a self-justifying logic to the adoption of a strategy that would enable its use.

During the Quebec Conference which began on 14 August 1943, Admiral King again stressed to the Allied planners present the importance of the Marianas to the war in the Pacific. Though the British, with an eye on the possible diversion of additional resources to Europe, suggested it might be prudent to adopt MacArthur's approach, the Combined Chiefs of Staff (CCS) sanctioned the forthcoming operations against the Gilberts and Marshalls. At this stage, however, the Marianas were only listed as a 'possible objective to be attacked, if necessary, when American forces had advanced to within striking distance'.

**Above:** A group photograph of Allied leaders on the terrace of the Citadel in Quebec, on the occasion of the First Quebec Conference, with Chateau Frontenac in the background. Seated, left to right, are: Canadian Prime Minister Mackenzie King; President Roosevelt; and Winston Churchill. Standing, again left to right, are: General H.H. Arnold, Chief of US Air Forces; Air Chief Marshal Sir Charles Portal; General Sir Alan Brooke, Chief of the Imperial General Staff; Admiral Ernest J. King, Chief of US Naval Forces; Field Marshal Sir John Dill; General George C. Marshall, Chief of Staff US Army; Sir Dudley Pound, Admiral of the Fleet and First Sea Lord; and Admiral W.D. Leahy, Chief of Staff to the Commander in Chief of the Navy. (NARA)

**Left:** Admiral Ernest J. King, a key proponent of operations against Saipan and the Marianas in general, pictured at the Navy Department between 1942 and 1944. (USNHHC)

With opinion divided, and to keep the persistently vocal MacArthur quiet, the CCS ultimately decided to support both thrusts, allowing MacArthur to advance towards the Philippines whilst initiating planning for King's attacks. It was the Sextant Conference, which opened on 22 November 1943, that resulted in a schedule of operations in the Pacific being drafted for planning purposes. This called for the invasion of the Marianas, the most heavily defended island of which was Saipan. The tentative date for this assault was set as 1 October 1944.

Any attack upon the Marianas would be vulnerable from aircraft operating out of Eniwetok Atoll, part of the Marshall Islands, where the Japanese had an airfield and a seaplane base. Likewise, if the US moved against Eniwetok its ships would be within striking distance of elements of the Imperial Japanese Navy's Combined Fleet stationed at its important forward base at Truk Lagoon. The first stage of the operation to take the Marianas therefore began with the bombing of the Japanese ships and warplanes at Truk.

Under the codename Operation *Hailstone*, three carrier task groups of Task Force 58, with more than 500 aircraft and seven battleships, attacked Truk on 17 February 1944, catching many of the defending 300 Japanese planes on the ground. The devastation was immense. Over the course of two days, more than forty warships and merchant ships were sunk, at least 250 aircraft were destroyed, and the anchorage's facilities were wrecked. Truk was abandoned by the Imperial Japanese Navy.

**Right:** Allied leaders pictured during the Cairo Conference, codenamed *Sextant*, on 25 November 1943. Left to right are Generalissimo Chiang Kai-shek, President Franklin D. Roosevelt, Prime Minister Winston Churchill, and Soong Mei-ling. (Historic Military Press)

**Above:** Japanese shipping under air attack in Truk Lagoon, as seen from a USS *Intrepid* (CV-11) aircraft on the first day of raids, 17 February 1944. Four ships in this picture appear to have been hit. (USNHHC)

**Right:** USS *New Jersey* (BB-62) steams past the burning debris of a Japanese ship destroyed during the US Navy's sweep around Truk, 16 February 1944. (NARA)

This attack was followed by an aerial assault upon the Marianas, to eliminate, or at least reduce, the powerful Japanese air force stationed there. The US Navy's Pacific Fleet could now turn its attention to Eniwetok without the threat of intervention from the Japanese.

The three islands of the Eniwetok Atoll were defended by 3,500 Japanese along with nine tanks and a few artillery pieces. It took the 22nd Marine Regiment and the 105th Infantry Regiment six days of hard fighting to take the islands, during which time almost all the Japanese defenders were killed.

The Pacific Fleet then had the base it needed for its assault upon the Marianas and a huge number of ships were gathered at Eniwetok for what was code-named Operation *Forager*. The fleet that finally departed from Eniwetok in early June 1944 was one of the largest assemblies of warships in maritime history.

**Right:** Admiral Nimitz inspects one of the first Boeing B-29 Superfortresses delivered to the Pacific area. It was the introduction of this aircraft that provided one of the central reasons for undertaking the landings on Saipan. (USNHHC)

**Above:** The battleship USS *New Mexico* (BB-40) at Eniwetok during late June 1944. The loading of 14-inch shells, from USS *Sangay* (AE-10), is underway in preparation for Operation *Forager*. (USNHHC)

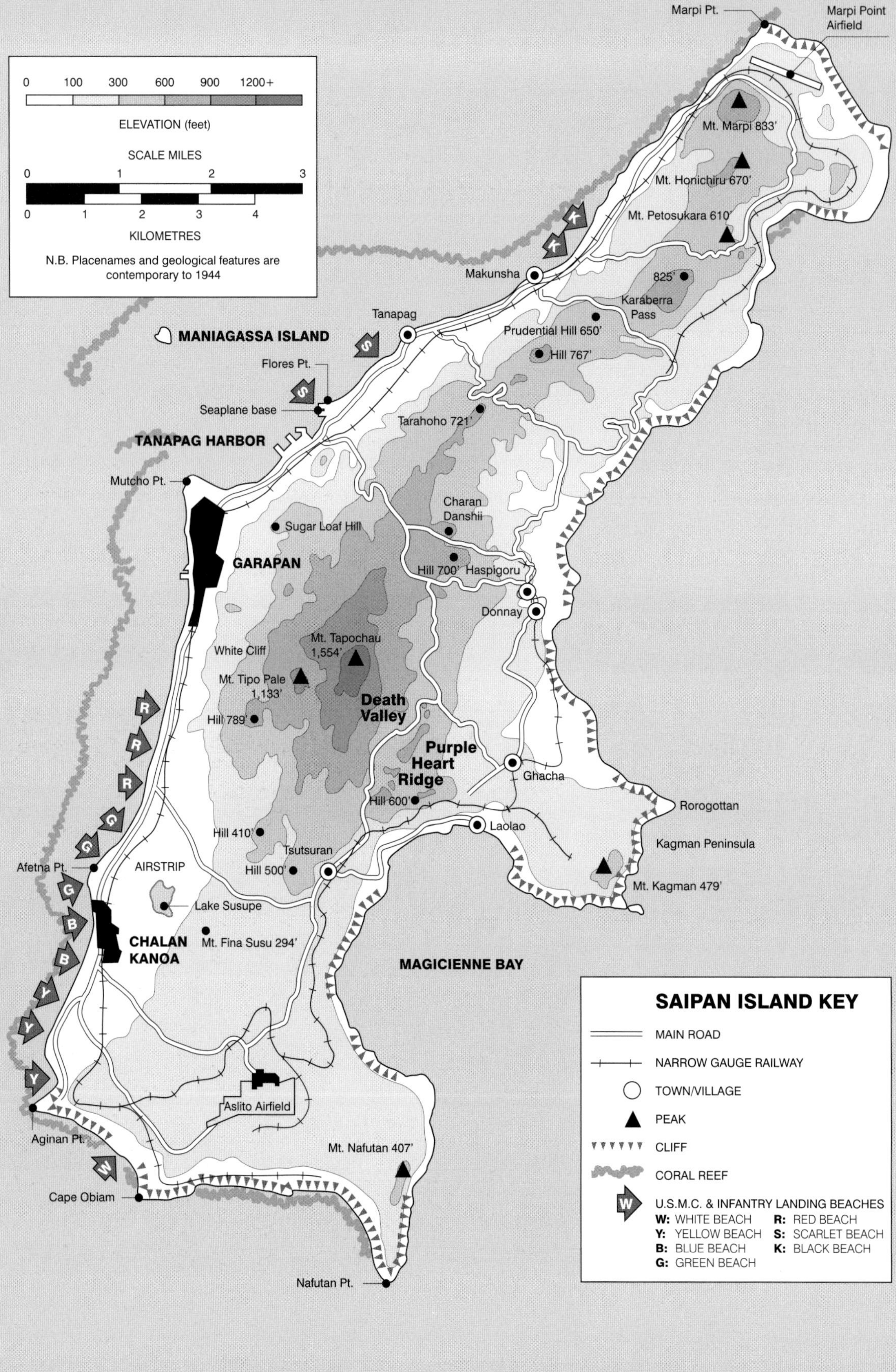
0 100 300 600 900 1200+
ELEVATION (feet)
SCALE MILES
0 1 2 3
0 1 2 3 4
KILOMETRES
N.B. Placenames and geological features are contemporary to 1944
Marpi Pt.
Marpi Point Airfield
Mt. Marpi 833'
Mt. Honichiru 670'
Mt. Petosukara 610'
Makunsha
825'
Karaberra Pass
Tanapag
Prudential Hill 650'
MANIAGASSA ISLAND
Hill 767'
Flores Pt.
Seaplane base
Tarahoho 721'
TANAPAG HARBOR
Mutcho Pt.
Charan Danshii
Sugar Loaf Hill
GARAPAN
Hill 700'
Haspigoru
Donnay
Mt. Tapochau 1,554'
White Cliff
Mt. Tipo Pale 1,133'
Death Valley
Hill 789'
Purple Heart Ridge
Ghacha
Hill 600'
Rorogottan
Laolao
Hill 410'
Kagman Peninsula
Tsutsuran
Afetna Pt.
AIRSTRIP
Hill 500'
Mt. Kagman 479'
Lake Susupe
CHALAN KANOA
Mt. Fina Susu 294'
MAGICIENNE BAY
Aslito Airfield
Aginan Pt.
Mt. Nafutan 407'
Cape Obiam
Nafutan Pt.
K
S
R
G
B
Y
W
SAIPAN ISLAND KEY
MAIN ROAD
NARROW GAUGE RAILWAY
TOWN/VILLAGE
PEAK
CLIFF
CORAL REEF
U.S.M.C. & INFANTRY LANDING BEACHES
W: WHITE BEACH
Y: YELLOW BEACH
B: BLUE BEACH
G: GREEN BEACH
R: RED BEACH
S: SCARLET BEACH
K: BLACK BEACH

Chapter 1

# THE PLAN OF ATTACK

The plan for Operation *Forager* was for a massive pre-emptive strike by carrier-borne aircraft on the Japanese airfields, followed by an intensive naval bombardment to neutralise the enemy's defences on all three main islands in the Marianas. Then the 2nd and 4th Marine Divisions would land on Saipan on 'D-Day'.

Three days later, Saipan having been secured, the 3rd Marine Division was to land on Guam. The US Army's 27th Infantry Division would remain embarked as a floating reserve to intervene on either island, should their help be required. Once Guam had been taken all attention could then be turned upon Tinian to complete the operation.

Admiral Raymond A. Spruance's US Fifth Fleet was divided into two main bodies, the Joint Expeditionary Force and Task Force 58. The Joint Expeditionary Force was sub-divided into the

**Below:** Ships of the Fifth Fleet at a Marshall Island anchorage, shortly before departure for the Marianas, as seen from USS *Gambier Bay* (CVE-73) on 10 June 1944. (USNHHC)

1

Northern Attack Force, which was to assault Saipan and Tinian, and the Southern Attack Force whose objective was Guam. Task Force 58 would provide the naval and aerial protection.

Saipan itself was captured by the Japanese in 1914. It was seized from Germany, which had, in turn, purchased Saipan from Spain in 1899 when the later set about disposing of her Pacific assets after the war with the United States. Formally handed control of the island in 1919 by the League of Nations, Japan soon established a sizeable civilian population.

Along with neighbouring Tinian, Saipan was closed to the world in 1933, with the result that when the American planners began work, little was known either of the defences or the enemy garrison. But as the islands had been Japanese for a generation, they were rightly considered legitimate Japanese territory. In assaulting these islands, for the first time in the war, the Americans would be fighting on Japanese soil.

The defence of the Marianas had not previously been a priority of the Japanese, despite being considered part of Japan's National Defence Zone. This was because until the loss of the Gilberts and the Marshalls, the Marianas had been far from the front line and had been used mainly as intermediate stations for the transit of troops to the outer regions of the empire. Vice-Chief of Staff Shigetarō Shimada was one officer who appreciated the importance of Saipan, as he made clear in a message to Prime Minister Tōjō on 18 June 1944: 'If we ever lose Saipan, repeated attacks on Tokyo will follow. No matter what it takes, we have to hold there.'[1]

**Right:** The light cruiser USS *Montpelier* and a destroyer en route from the Marshall Islands to take part in the invasion of Saipan on 11 June 1944. This picture was taken from the escort carrier USS *Gambier Bay*. (USNHHC)

Despite Shimada's warning, the view taken by the Imperial Navy's General Staff was that the main US move would be the thrust by MacArthur towards the Philippines. By the time Tokyo realised that the Marianas were likely to be threatened, it was already too late to retrieve the situation.

As late as February 1944, there were less than 1,500 troops on Saipan and when the Japanese high command belatedly awoke to the danger that the island was in, hurried attempts were made to reinforce the garrison and prepare for its defence. Though more than 45,000 troops were shipped to the Marianas, not all were destined to arrive. The submarine USS *Trout* sank the troop transport *Sakito Maru* on the last day of February (though *Trout* itself was sunk by escorting warships), with the loss of 2,400 men. Five other transports were also sent to the bottom, taking with them most of the Japanese 118th Regiment. Those that survived the sinking of the transport and managed to reach Saipan, struggled ashore without their weapons. Altogether, nine transports were sunk en route, resulting in the loss of more than 3,600 men and much military equipment and construction materials.

Nevertheless, around tens of thousands of men reached the Marianas. This, though, was not immediately known to the US planners. On 9 May 1944, one assessment declared that no more than 10,000 Japanese were stationed at Saipan. By the eve of the invasion, this figure had soared to 15,000-17,600. This final estimate included 9,100-11,000 combat troops, 900-1,200 aviation personnel, 1,600-1,900 Japanese labourers, some 400-500 Koreans, and 3,000 'home guards'. The latter described as 'recent recruits who were believed to be the scrapings from the bottom of the manpower barrel'. The actual number of Japanese was approximately 30,000 soldiers and sailors plus hundreds of civilians, though even this number varies between sources.

Those defenders who had reached the Marianas were immediately put to work constructing defences. However, when the Americans attacked, many fortifications were incomplete and much of their heavy weaponry was still unmounted or in storage.

In command of the recently created Central Area Pacific Fleet was Admiral Chūichi Nagumo, the man who had commanded the Carrier Striking Force which attacked Pearl Harbor. He was also the man who had seen that same force destroyed at the Battle of Midway in 1942 and was no longer viewed by many as a capable leader. He was given command in the region because the central Pacific had been considered safe from enemy attention.

It was Lieutenant General Hideyoshi Obata, in command of the Japanese 31st Army, who was responsible for the defence of the Marianas. Defending Saipan itself was Lieutenant General Yoshitsugu Saitō's 43rd Infantry Division and Colonel Yoshiro Oka's Independent Mixed Brigade. There were also in excess of 6,000 naval personnel under Nagumo on the island, as well as an anti-aircraft company, various engineering regiments, a considerable number of artillery pieces and mortars, as well as forty-eight tanks. The total number of troops on the island amounted to almost 32,000 – far more than the Americans had estimated. But many of these had reached the island in a disorganised state because of the sinking of so many transports and not all the assorted units had been fully integrated into the island's defensive command structure.

The island of Saipan is 12.5 miles long and varies in width between 2.5 and 5.5 miles. As one official history of the US Marine Corps notes, 'no single adjective can glibly describe the irregularly shaped island of Saipan'. The authors went on to state: 'Three outcroppings, Agingan Point, Cape

**Left:** Transports in convoy en route from Espiritu Santo, New Hebrides, for Kwajalein to stage on to the Marianas, in early June 1944. This photograph was taken from USS *Pocomoke* (AV-9) which provided patrol seaplane support for the operation. (USNHHC)

**Main image:** Battleships and escort carriers of Task Force 52 en route to Saipan in early June 1944. The battleships are USS *Idaho* and USS *Pennsylvania*. (USNHHC)

Obiam, and Nafutan Point, mar the profile of the southern coast. The western shoreline of Saipan extends almost due north from Agingan Point past the town of Charan Kanoa, past Afetna Point and the city of Garapan [the capital] to Mutcho Point. Here, midway along the island, the coastline veers to the northeast, curving slightly to embrace Tanapag Harbor and finally terminating at rugged Marpi Point.

'The eastern shore wends its sinuous way southward from Marpi Point, beyond the Kagman Peninsula and Magicienne Bay, to the rocks of Nafutan Point. Cliffs guard most of the eastern and southern beaches from Marpi Point to Cape Obiam. There is a gap in this barrier inland of Magicienne Bay, but a reef, located close inshore, serves to hinder small craft. Although the western beaches are comparatively level, a reef extends from the vicinity of Marpi Point to an opening off Tanapag Harbor, then continues, though broken by several gaps, to Agingan Point.'[2]

Saipan has a total land mass of approximately 72 square miles.[3] Saipan's highest point, at 1,553 feet, is Mount Tapochau (also spelt Tapotchau, or even Topotchau in some accounts) in the centre of the island. It is part of a range of heights which runs to Mount Marpi at the northern tip of the island and southwards to the 1,133-foot Mount Tipo Pale. These heights were then, and still are, covered in dense vegetation and pock-marked with caves and broken by deep ravines and valleys. There are just two significant urban areas, both

**Right:** Ships of Fire Support Group 2 (Task Group 52.10) under Rear Admiral W.L. Ainsworth, en route to Saipan after departing Roi Island on 12 June 1944. This picture was taken from USS *Honolulu*. The other ships are, from left to right, *St. Louis* (CL-49), *Wichita* (CA-45), *Minneapolis* (CA-36), *San Francisco* (CA-38) and *New Orleans* (CA-32), as well as the battleships *Idaho* (BB-42), *Pennsylvania* (BB-38), and *New Mexico*. (USNHHC)

situated on the western coast, the capital, Garapan, and a smaller town situated three to four miles further south, Chalan Kanoa.

It was near here that the Japanese had built a 3,280-foot runway on one airfield, with, further south still, one of 3,600-foot on a second airfield at Aslito (this is today the site of Saipan International Airport). There was also a seaplane base near Tanapag Harbour, the island's main port. Tanapag Harbor is separated from the Philippine Sea by a barrier reef which forms the Saipan Lagoon. There were approximately 152 aircraft stationed on the island.

The plan of attack as visualised by Lieutenant General Holland McTyeire Smith, the commander of V Amphibious Corps, was to assault the south-western coast of Saipan along a 1,000-yard stretch of shoreline divided into four landing beaches, designated Red, Green, Blue and Yellow. The 2nd Marine Division was to attack the northern beaches, with the 6th Regiment taking Red Beach and the 8th taking Green, while the 23rd and 25th regiments of the 4th Marine Division in the south assaulted Blue and Yellow respectively.

Once established ashore, the 2nd Division was to turn northwards while the 4th Division moved eastwards and then pivoted on the flank of the 2nd Division to swing northwards. Together, the two marine divisions would push towards the northern end of the island, destroying the enemy as they went. The entire operation was expected to take three days.

That, at least, was the plan. The reality, as was so often the case during the war in the Pacific, proved far different. When it happened, in June and July 1944, the conquest of Saipan became the 'most daring – and disturbing – operation'[4] in America's war against Japan to date.

**Right:** The Fletcher-class destroyer USS *Terry* (DD-513) departing the island of Roi to take part in the invasion of Saipan, 12 June 1944. (USNHHC)

**Above:** Ships of Task Force 52 prepare to depart Roi for Saipan on 12 June 1944, as seen from USS *New Mexico*. They are, from left to right, USS *McNair* (DD-679), USS *Montpelier* (CL-57), USS *Honolulu* (CL-48) and the battleship USS *Tennessee* (BB-43). (NARA)

Chapter 2

# PRELIMINARY OPERATIONS

Such was the Allies' progress in the Pacific theatre that the Marianas were soon selected as the next objective in the Central Pacific campaign. Once again, the major factor that influenced American planners was the continuing and pressing need for bases from which the new B-29s could launch their offensive against the Japanese homeland. It was on 20 March 1944, that Admiral King issued instructions for the formal planning of Operation *Forager* to begin. D-Day was set for 15 June 1944.

On 6 June, while the ships carrying the invasion force headed westward for their staging bases in the Marshall Islands, ahead of them Admiral Marc Mitscher's Task Force 58 weighed anchor and slipped out of Majuro, the capital and largest city of the Marshall Islands, for waters to the east of

**Above:** With the US Navy having so little knowledge of Saipan, detailed reconnaissance was essential, but this had to be undertaken with great care. If the Japanese realised that the Marianas were the next US target, rather than MacArthur's move northwards, the Japanese might attempt to concentrate their fleet in a bid to reverse the results of the battles of Midway and Coral Sea. American carrier aircraft, therefore, undertook photographic reconnaissance flights only once in February, April and May. The submarine USS *Greenling* (SS-213), seen here, managed to take good photographs of parts of the island in April. This photograph was taken on 17 May 1943, presumably while the submarine was leaving Brisbane, Australia, for her sixth war patrol – this being the one in which she completed her reconnaissance of Saipan. (USNHHC)

**Above:** The aircraft carrier USS *Belleau Wood* (CVL-24) pictured from USS *Essex* (CV-9) during the attacks on Japanese positions on Saipan on 22 February 1944. (National Museum of the US Navy)

**Left:** On 22 February 1944, a major attack was delivered by US carrier aircraft which bombed installations at Saipan, Guam and Tinian. It is stated that more than 135 Japanese fighters and bombers were destroyed. In this photograph, Japanese planes, including A6M Zeros and G4M Betty bombers, burn on what is probably Aslito airfield. (USNHHC)

the Marianas. For this deployment Mitscher had assembled an armada that included a total of seven aircraft carriers, eight light carriers, seven fast battleships, three heavy cruisers, ten light cruisers, and fifty-two destroyers. This formidable gathering of warships had one main task – the preliminary subjugation of the Marianas.

The first step of this naval bombardment of the islands was to be an aerial assault scheduled for first light on 12 June. Good weather and excellent planning and preparation found Mitscher's aircrews ready and in position earlier than expected. As a result, permission was sought, and duly granted, for the first fighter sweep to be launched on the afternoon of 11 June. It was

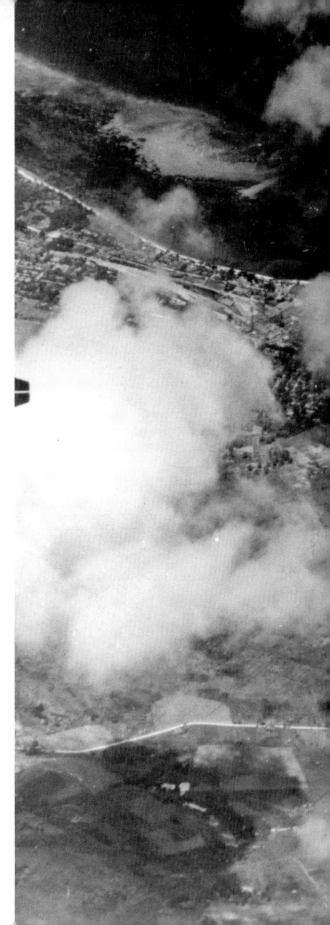

**Above:** A Japanese Yokosuka D4Y 'Judy' bomber pictured from USS *Essex* as it dived towards the carrier during the US raid on Saipan by Task Group 58.2 on 22 February 1944. (National Museum of the US Navy)

**Right:** An aerial reconnaissance photograph of the Charan Kanoa area on Saipan, showing reef, lagoon and airstrip from the air, that was taken on 29 May 1944. (USNHHC)

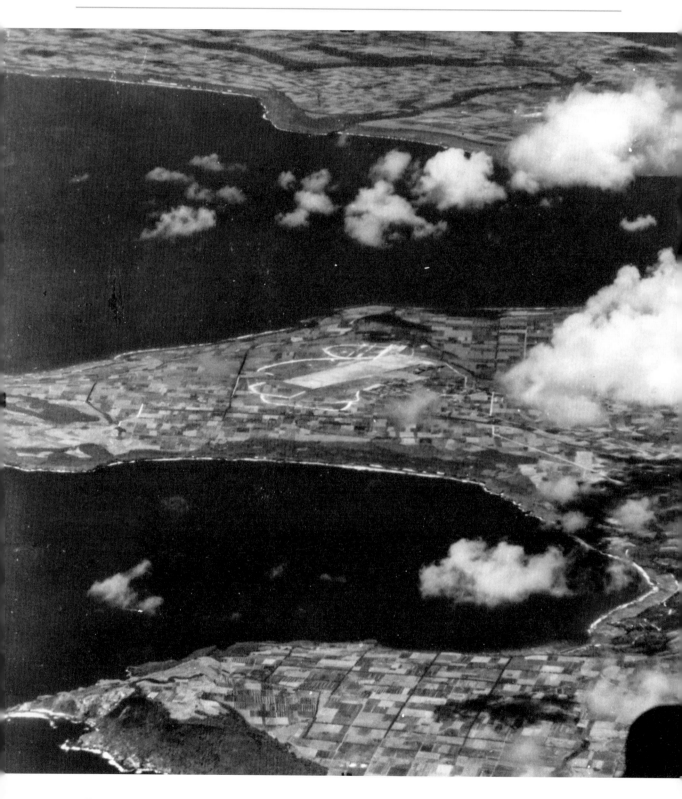

at 13.00 hours that afternoon when the first planes took off from the carriers, at which point Task Force 58 was approximately 192 miles north-east of Guam and 225 miles south-east of Saipan and Tinian.

The results were, noted the historian Philip A. Crowl, 'altogether gratifying': 'Of the 225 planes launched in this initial fighter sweep, only twelve were lost. By contrast, the enemy suffered heavily. Estimates as to Japanese aircraft put out of operation either through destruction or serious damage ran from 147 to 215.'[5] At no time following this attack were Japanese land-based aircraft more than a minor nuisance to American operations in the area.

Matsuya Tokuzo, serving in the 9th Tank Regiment, described being on the receiving end of this strike in his diary: 'At a little after 1300, I was awakened by the air raid alarm and immediately led all men into the trench. Scores of enemy Grumman fighters began strafing and bombing Aslito airfield and Garapan. For about two hours, the enemy planes ran amuck and finally left leisurely amidst the ... inaccurate anti-aircraft fire. All we could do was watch helplessly. At night we went to extinguish the mountain fires which had been caused by gun fire. They were finally brought completely under control.'

Despite the severity of the attack, ashore on Saipan Lieutenant General Saitō and his staff failed to grasp its implications. They erroneously assumed that far from being the precursor to a full-blown amphibious Allied landing, it was just another fighter sweep. What followed over the next few days would, however, quickly dispel any doubts as to the Americans' intentions.

For three days, all four of Mitscher's task groups pounded the main islands in the Marianas. Everything was a target – the few surviving Japanese aircraft, airfields, coastal defence batteries, anti-aircraft positions, and command posts were all hit. Even the sugar cane fields south of Mutcho Point on Saipan were set alight to aid the landing troops.

Then, on 13 June, a designated naval bombardment group, comprising seven fast battleships and eleven designated destroyers, first unleashed their guns on the Japanese defenders. From 10.40 hours until about 17.25 hours they pounded the west coasts of Saipan and Tinian, even as the aerial onslaught raged on unabated.

The diary of one unnamed Japanese soldier, found after the invasion, provides an insight into what it was like to be on the receiving end of this devastating combined bombardment: 'At 0500 there was a fierce enemy air attack. I have at last come to the place where I will die. I am pleased to think that I will die calmly in true samurai style. Naval gunfire supported this attack which was too terrible for words. I feel now like a full-fledged warrior. Towards evening the firing died down but at night naval gunfire continued as before.'

One Japanese naval officer recalled how, 'the shells began to fall closer and closer to the airfield'. 'It was frightful,' he wrote in conclusion.

By the morning of 14 June, the reality of what was about to happen had finally been recognised by Saitō and his men. That day, the following message was sent by the garrison to the 31st Army headquarters: 'Since early this morning the enemy small vessels have been planting markers and searching for tank passages on the reef. Because as far as one can see there are no transports, the landing will have to be after tonight or dawn tomorrow.'[6] It was, as events would soon show, an entirely correct assessment.

**Left:** This aerial reconnaissance photograph, also taken on 29 May 1944, shows Magicienne Bay and Aslito Field at Saipan. In the distance is the island of Tinian. (USNHHC)

**Above:** A Japanese cargo ship, probably *Nitcho Maru*, capsized and sinking off Saipan on 12 June 1944. She was hit by an aircraft from USS *Enterprise* (CV-6), more specifically that flown by Lieutenant Junior Grade S.S. McCrary. (USNHHC)

**Below:** A Japanese shore battery straddles the cruiser USS *Birmingham* (CL-62) during the US Navy's preliminary bombardment of Saipan. (USNHHC)

**Above:** The preliminary naval bombardment of Saipan was to begin on D-2 with the arrival of fast battleships and destroyers from Task Force 58. Taken by an aircraft from USS *Lexington* (CV-16), this photograph shows battleships and cruisers manoeuvring off Saipan and Tinian on 14 June. (USNHHC)

**Below:** A view of Japanese ships in Tanapag Harbor, Saipan. This photograph was taken by aircraft operating from USS *Wasp* (CV-7) during attacks by Task Force 58. (USNHHC)

**Above:** On 14 June, approximately 200 divers of the Navy's Underwater Demolition Teams (UDTs), half of whom were under the command of Commander L. Kauffman and half under Lieutenant Richard F. Burke, were sent to scout out the landing beaches. A third team, of some eighty men, examined the area north of Tanapag Harbor. All the men in the UDTs were naval personnel except for one Army and one Marine liaison officer per team. Here can be seen a landing craft from USS *Clemson* (DD-186) launching a rubber raft for a UDT party. (NARA)

**Left:** US warships of Task Force 52 mass off Saipan in preparation for the invasion, as seen from a fast transport carrying one of the Underwater Demolition Teams. Veteran Clarence McDuffie, serving in the 538th Port Company, vividly recalls the sight of the invasion force, though he had no idea at the time just where he was headed: 'When you see all the different ships and destroyers and escorts … heading in the same direction, as far as your eyes can behold, east, west, north, south, behind you, in front of you, that's when you realize you're going somewhere. [That] something big's going to happen.'[7] (USNHHC)

**Right:** Members of Underwater Demolition Team Six pictured boarding a landing craft off Saipan. Among their tasks, UDT divers swam ashore to measure the height of the barrier reef off the landing beaches, the depth of the water, and the distance between the reef and the beach as well as checking for any underwater obstacles. This mission was undertaken during daylight hours and was spotted by the Japanese who then knew where the Marines were going to land. This enabled the defenders to plant flags at various intervals in the water and on the reef to help sight their artillery. (NARA)

**Above:** Underwater Demolition Team personnel working on the barrier reef. Other UDT men can be seen around a rubber raft to the right of the photograph. The men were transported from the destroyers in small boats to the edge of the reef, from where they swam close into the shoreline in full daylight under the protection of ships' fire. (NARA)

**Above:** Underwater demolition team members pass explosive charges from a landing craft to a rubber raft, during clearance operations off Saipan in June 1944. The UDTs performed their work under considerable fire from the beach, but despite this only two men were killed and fifteen wounded. (NARA)

**Right:** Units of Cruiser Division Six bombard Saipan on 14-15 June 1944. The nearest ship is USS *New Orleans*. Beyond her is USS *St. Louis*. The preliminary bombardment did not achieve all of its aims. A Japanese artillery instructor, assigned to Saipan as an observer, managed to radio the following report on the effects of the shelling: 'Each [of the] positions withstood four days of bombardment. Those observation posts and gun emplacements that were protected by splinter-proof shelters were able to withstand the bombardment. Dummy positions proved very effective. During bombardment, both day and night, movement to alternate positions was very difficult. Communication lines were cut frequently, and the need for repairs and messengers was great.' (USNHHC)

**Above:** Underwater demolition team blows up an obstacle off the beaches of Saipan near several LSTs. *LST-390* is identifiable at the right. Generally speaking, particularly at the start of the US landings, almost no obstacles were reported and hence virtually no demolition work was necessary. (NARA)

**Above:** The cruiser USS *Honolulu*, on the left, and a destroyer in the waters between Saipan and Tinian on 14 June, the first day of bombardment by Task Group 52, as seen from USS *New Mexico*. (USNHHC)

**Below:** The cruiser USS *Louisville* (CA-28) moves in close to the beaches at Saipan in order to support the invasion, 14-15 June. (US Navy)

**Above:** A burning Japanese cargo ship attacked by planes from USS *Lexington* on 14 June. (USNHHC)

**Below:** Japanese prisoners under guard aboard USS *Enterprise* after their ship had been bombed and sunk by Task Force 58 planes during operations near Saipan on 14 June. (USNHHC)

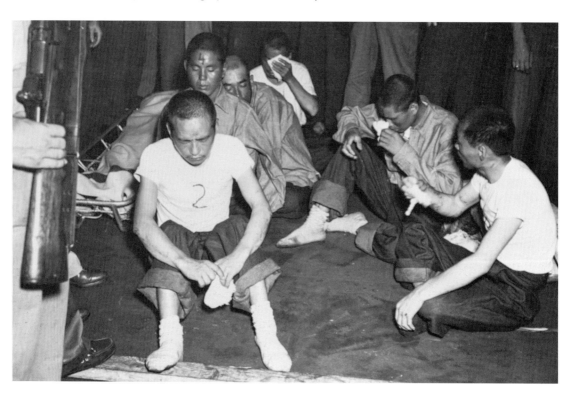

**Above:** Huge pillars of smoke rise into the sky as fires rage at a fuel dump (left of centre) and the Charan Kanoa sugar refinery (right) during US air strikes on Saipan in June 1944. (USNHHC)

**Below:** The pre-invasion bombardment of Saipan on 14 June kicks up dust and smoke. (USNHHC)

Chapter 3

# D-DAY

15 June 1944

As the minutes ticked down to the invasion, the Fire Support Group, consisting of the battleships *Tennessee* and *California* (BB-44), the cruisers *Birmingham* and *Indianapolis* (CA-35), and the destroyers *Norman Scott* (DD-690), *Monssen* (DD-436), *Coghlan* (DD-606), *Halsey Powell* (DD-686), *Bailey* (DD-492), *Robinson* (DD-562), and *Albert W. Grant* (DD-649), took up positions less than 2,500 yards from the shore on Saipan. Then, at 04.30 hours on D-Day, 15 June 1944, they opened fire directly at the landing beach areas.

Their bombardment ceased at 06.30 hours to allow the US Navy's aircraft to open their account. That came when fifty fighters, fifty-one dive bombers and fifty-four torpedo bombers struck Japanese positions around the landing beaches.

**Below:** Ahead of the landing forces early on the morning of 15 June, twenty-four LCI(G)s (Landing Craft, Infantry, Gunboats) armed with 4.5-inch rockets and 20mm and 40mm guns, rushed towards the barrier reef to lay down a supressing fire upon the beach. Behind them were the amphibious tanks (Landing Vehicle Tanks, or LVTs) with their turret-mounted 75mm howitzers. In this photograph US Marine Corps LVTs head for the shore as part of the first wave of the US landings on Saipan on 15 June 1944. (USNHHC)

**Above:** A Douglas SBD Dauntless from USS *Lexington* flies over Tanapag Harbor, Saipan, during the landings on 15 June 1944. (USNHHC)

**Above:** Part of the invasion force in the assault transport area off Saipan on 15 June – as seen from another Dauntless operating from USS *Lexington*. (USNHHC)

'At 0545,' noted Philip A. Crowl, 'the word was passed throughout the American task forces that H-Hour, the moment at which the first troops were supposed to land, would be 0830 hours, as scheduled. Guns and winches were manned; boats were lowered into the water from the transports.

'Shortly after 0700 the thirty-four LSTs carrying the Marine assault battalions moved into position, and dropped anchor about half a mile off the line of departure. The line, the starting point from which the assault landing craft would take off, was located 4,250 yards offshore. Bow doors swung open; ramps lowered, and hundreds of amphibian tractors and amphibian tanks crawled into the water and commenced to circle. In all, 719 of these craft would be employed in the operation.'

However, the unloading of the amphibious vehicles took longer than anticipated. Consequently, at 07.50 hours the decision was taken to delay H-Hour by ten minutes. Then, at 08.12 hours, the first wave set off, motors roaring, towards the shore.

Other problems were soon encountered. For example, a strong current pushed the transports carrying the 2nd Marine Division too far to the north, leaving a gap of some 400 yards between it

**Above:** Dauntless dive bombers from USS *Lexington* fly over Saipan on their way to bomb Aslito airfield on D-Day. (USNHHC)

and the 4th Division. This only added to the confusion generated by the hail of bullets from small arms and machine-guns, and bombs and shells from mortars and well-sited artillery the preparatory bombardment had been unable to silence.

So heavy was the fire of the defenders, the two divisions were unable to bridge the gap and make contact as they slowly battled their way inland. At the same time, trees, trenches, and shell holes stopped some of the tanks of the 2nd Armored Amphibian Battalion before they could even cross the beach.

'All around us was the chaotic debris of bitter combat,' recalled 1st Lieutenant John C. Chapin of the 3rd Battalion, 24th Marines. 'Jap and Marine bodies lying in mangled and grotesque positions; blasted and burnt-out pillboxes; the burning wrecks of LVTs that had been knocked out by Jap high velocity fire; the acrid smell of high explosives; the shattered trees; and the churned-up sand littered with discarded equipment.'[8]

After more than two hours of fighting, the Marines had only advanced a few hundred yards inland – much of that distance on their bellies. 'It's hard to dig a hole when you're lying on your stomach digging with your chin, your elbows, your knees, and your toes,' mused one Marine. Yet, as he concluded, 'it is possible'.[9]

But, from 13.00 hours, the first of the 2nd Division's tanks had landed on Green Beach and moved northward to support the 6th Marines. By the middle of the afternoon those tanks assigned to the 8th Marines had also successfully landed and were soon in operation. The tide of battle was beginning to turn.

By nightfall, the invaders had established a beachhead approximately 10,000 yards in length and over 1,000 yards in depth in most places. Two divisions were ashore with almost all their reserves, as were the majority of the survivors of the two tank battalions.

**Above:** Some of USS *Lexington*'s Dauntless dive bombers fly over the invasion fleet off Saipan. (USNHHC)

**Right:** Commander William R. 'Killer' Kane, USS *Enterprise*'s air group commander, is returned to his ship after being shot down over Saipan while directing air strikes. The destroyer is probably USS *Patterson* (DD-392). Commander Kane survived the war, only to be killed, aged 45, in a plane crash in February 1957. At the time he was the commander of the US Navy's aircraft carrier USS *Saipan*. (US Navy)

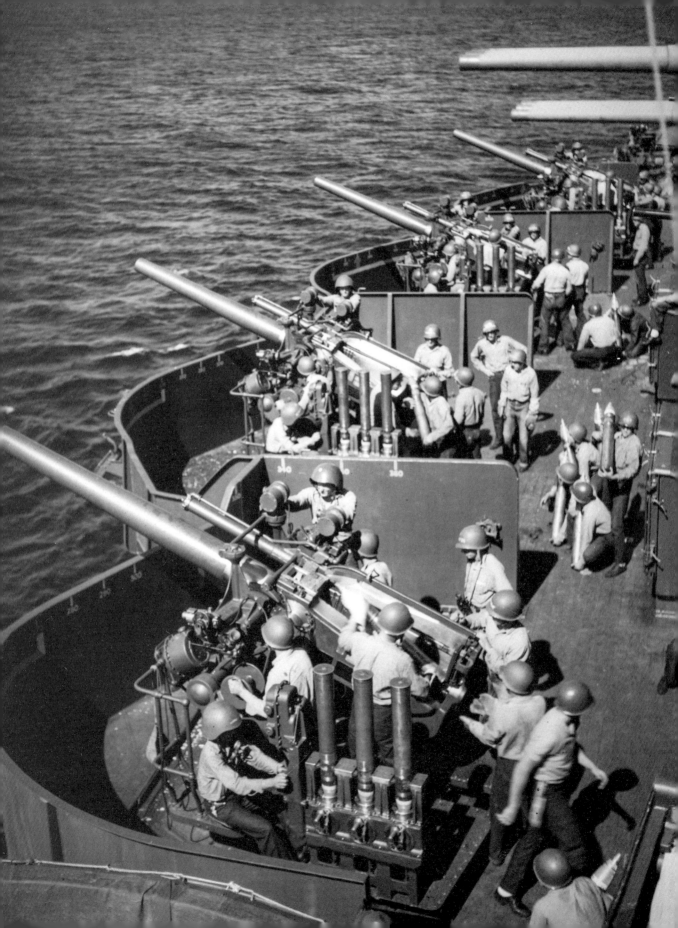

**Left:** At about 07.00 hours the supporting US warships recommenced their bombardment. In this photograph the 5/25-inch battery of USS *New Mexico*, of Fire Support Group 2, prepares to participate in the bombardment on 15 June. (USNHHC)

**Below:** In action off Saipan – USS *New Mexico*'s 5.25-inch guns open fire. (US Navy)

**Left:** The battleship USS *New Mexico* firing in support of the landings on Saipan. Another battleship, USS *Pennsylvania*, can be seen in the background. Note that the middle gun in *New Mexico*'s No.3 turret is in the recoil position. (USNHHC)

**Above:** Lieutenant General Holland M. Smith USMC (left) with Vice-Admiral Richmond K. Turner USN on board the Appalachian-class command ship USS *Rocky Mount* (AGC-3) at H-Hour on D-Day. *Rocky Mount* sailed for Saipan on 29 May as the flagship for the Joint Expeditionary Force attacking the Marianas Islands. She reached Saipan on 15 June, being used to direct the initial landings. (US Navy)

**Top left:** Lieutenant General Holland M. Smith USMC studies maps and aerial reconnaissance photographs of Saipan, 15 June 1944. (USMC Archives)

**Bottom left:** A pair of Landing Craft Infantry (Gun), more specifically LCI(G) 725 and LCI(G) 726, fire on one of the target beaches while a veritable armada of landing craft and LVTs forms up in the background during the initial assault. (NARA)

**Above:** LVTs and landing craft move toward the beaches on Saipan, past bombarding cruisers, on 15 June. The cruiser firing in the background is USS *Indianapolis*, Admiral Spruance's flagship. This photograph was taken from USS *Birmingham*. (USNHHC)

**Overleaf:** The landings on Saipan underway, captured in this dramatic picture showing Marines of the first wave ashore hugging the beach and preparing to move inland on D-Day. An LVT, hit by Japanese fire, can be seen burning in the background. (NARA)

**Above:** The scene on one of the beachheads on Saipan as Marines dig in, creating some shelter, before attempting to press on inland. (National Museum of the US Navy)

**Left:** One of the most iconic images of the Battle of Saipan, this picture shows US Marines stumbling having been hit by enemy fire as they storm ashore. Note that these Marines are all armed with M-1 carbines. (NARA)

**Below:** The same spot, to the south of Garapan, during a recent visit. (John Grehan Collection)

**Left:** Men of the first wave of Marines to go ashore on Saipan shelter behind a sand dune. (NARA)

**Below:** Marines shelter on one of the beaches during the landings in Saipan. A strong current pushed the boats carrying the 2nd Marine Division too far to the north, leaving a gap of some 400 yards between it and the 4th Division. This added to the confusion on the beaches generated by the hail of bullets from small arms and machine-guns, and bombs and shells from mortars and well-sited artillery the Navy had been unable to silence. So heavy was the fire of the defenders, the two divisions were unable to bridge the gap and make contact as they slowly made their way inland. Trees, trenches, and shell holes stopped some of the tanks of the 2nd Armored Amphibian Battalion before they could even cross the beach. (USMC Archives)

**Right:** Marines crawling into position on the beach after their landing craft was hit by a Japanese mortar. Note the LVT(A)-4 in the background. (USMC Archives)

**Above:** Part of one of the landing beaches as it appears today – in this case, as the information panel informs the visitor, it is a stretch of what was Yellow Beach. This was the most southerly of the landing beaches on Saipan on 15 June 1944. The sign states: 'Heavy Japanese fire pinned down the three regiments of the U.S. 4th Marine Division that stormed this beach on the morning of Thursday June 15, 1944. To make their way up the first 12 yards of Yellow Beach took the Marines a full hour of heavy fighting.' (John Grehan Collection)

**Main image:** The tanks suffered severely on D-Day, from both the intense enemy fire and the problems they encountered crossing the reef and a variety of obstacles on the beach. Mechanical failure also took its toll, so that by the end of the first day of battle the 2nd Marine Division had only thirteen operational tanks out of the seventy which had been assigned to it. This photograph, taken on 16 June, is of the wrecked LVTs and other debris on one of the invasion beaches. (USMC Archives).

**Top left:** An oil painting by the war artist Robert Benney depicts Marines in action after hitting the beach on 15 June. One of the Marines is equipped with a flamethrower. (USNHHC)

**Bottom left:** A wrecked Japanese coastal defence gun emplacement on Saipan that was captured by Marines. The gun is supposedly a British-made 6-inch piece, possibly removed from Singapore after its capture by Japanese forces. (USNHHC)

**Above:** To prevent 'friendly fire' which might be caused by over-shooting from rifles during the confusion of the landings, some of the Marine units were issued with shotguns. All the shotguns allocated to the 8th Marines had been handed to Captain (later Major) Carl Hoffman's Company G of the 2nd Battalion, which landed on Green 2 Beach. This gave the company a ratio of one shotgun for every two Marines, who also carried their regulation weapons. 'We were glad we were armed with shotguns,' noted Hoffman, 'because the entire beach that we were moving along was a honeycomb of World War I-type open trenches. The Japanese were in these open trenches and had survived the bombardment from naval gunfire. And they were ready to fight. So we had a lot of hand-to-hand fighting, and there's nothing more effective in hand-to-hand fighting than shotguns ... Many of the Japanese were ready to do battle with bayonets or even sabres.'[10] This photograph gives some indication of the conditions on the beaches. (USMC Archives)

**Top left:** A surviving Japanese pillbox on the edge of what was Blue Beach on Saipan, and which was attacked by the 4th Marine Division's 23rd Regiment during the landings on 15 June 1944. (John Grehan Collection)

**Bottom left:** African American Marines preparing to move off the beach shortly after landing on Saipan. One of the African American Marine units ashore on D-Day was the 20th Marine Depot Company. It landed on Yellow Beach 2, in support of the 1st Battalion, 25th Marines, 4th Marine Division. Captain William C. Adams, the company commander, later recalled the following: 'My company landed about 2 p.m. on D-Day. We were the third wave, and all hell was breaking when we came in. It was still touch and go when we hit shore, and it took some time to establish a foothold. My men performed excellently … They did a swell job … Among my own company casualties, my orderly was killed.' Adams' orderly was Private First Class [Pfc] Kenneth J. Tibbs, who suffered fatal wounds and died the same day. Aged 19, he was the first African American Marine killed in combat during the Second World War. (NARA)

**Below:** The ruins of another, in this case incomplete, Japanese coastal gun position after its capture by the Marines who landed on Saipan. (USNHHC)

**Right:** A knocked-out Japanese Type 95 *Ha-Gō* light tank at one of the invasion beaches on Saipan. (National Museum of the US Navy)

**Above:** A US serviceman inspects a captured Japanese artillery piece on Saipan. As his men battled inland from the beachheads, 1st Lieutenant John C. Chapin, of the 3rd Battalion, 24th Marines, recalled being on the receiving end of the enemy guns: 'Suddenly, WHAM! A shell hit right on top of us! I was too surprised to think, but instinctively all of us hit the deck and began to spread out. Then the shells really began to pour down on us: ahead, behind, on both sides, and right in our midst. They would come rocketing down with a freight-train roar and then explode with a deafening cataclysm that is beyond description.'[11] (National Museum of the US Navy)

**Above:** The scene on one of the landing beaches on Saipan on D-Day, 15 June 1944. (NARA)

**Right:** By nightfall on 15 June, the two Marine divisions had succeeded in establishing themselves on the western coast of Saipan. Approximately half of the planned beachhead had been won, but the Japanese defenders still held the ridges that dominated captured segments of the coastal plain. Although no accurate accounting was made until 17 June, as many as 2,000 men may have been killed or wounded on D-Day.[12] The view here is of the town of Charan Kanoa and the invasion beaches, taken from the surrounding hills a few days after the invasion.(USNHHC)

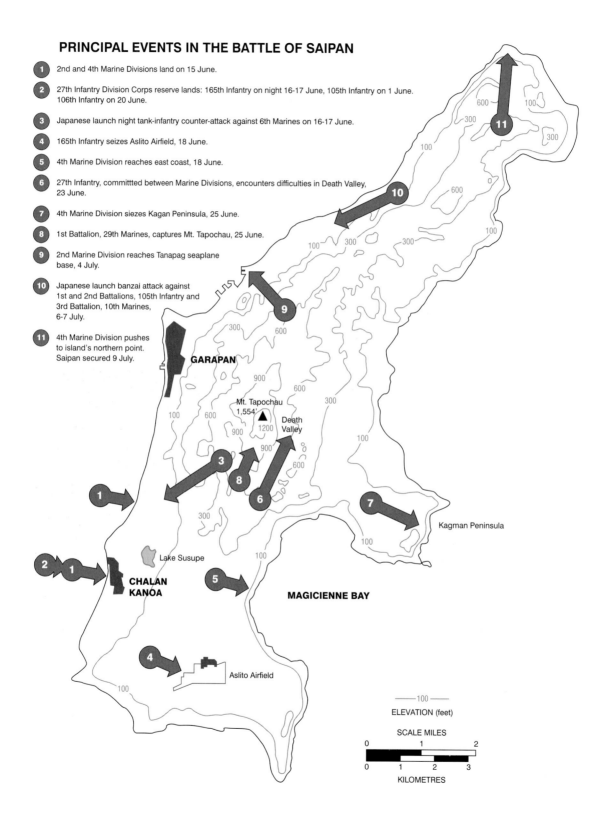

# PRINCIPAL EVENTS IN THE BATTLE OF SAIPAN

1. 2nd and 4th Marine Divisions land on 15 June.

2. 27th Infantry Division Corps reserve lands: 165th Infantry on night 16-17 June, 105th Infantry on 1 June. 106th Infantry on 20 June.

3. Japanese launch night tank-infantry counter-attack against 6th Marines on 16-17 June.

4. 165th Infantry seizes Aslito Airfield, 18 June.

5. 4th Marine Division reaches east coast, 18 June.

6. 27th Infantry, committted between Marine Divisions, encounters difficulties in Death Valley, 23 June.

7. 4th Marine Division siezes Kagan Peninsula, 25 June.

8. 1st Battalion, 29th Marines, captures Mt. Tapochau, 25 June.

9. 2nd Marine Division reaches Tanapag seaplane base, 4 July.

10. Japanese launch banzai attack against 1st and 2nd Battalions, 105th Infantry and 3rd Battalion, 10th Marines, 6-7 July.

11. 4th Marine Division pushes to island's northern point. Saipan secured 9 July.

GARAPAN

Mt. Tapochau
1,554'

Death Valley

Kagman Peninsula

Lake Susupe

CHALAN KANOA

MAGICIENNE BAY

Aslito Airfield

—— 100 ——
ELEVATION (feet)

SCALE MILES
0    1    2

0    1    2    3
KILOMETRES

Chapter 4

# INTO THE MOUNTAINS

**Above:** During the first night of the invasion, the Japanese continued to shell the still precarious positions held by the Marines. This bombardment, though, was merely the prelude to what was to be a counter-attack aimed at sweeping the Americans back into the sea. For this, Saitō had at his command forty-four tanks of Colonel Goto's 9th Tank Regiment, twelve of which were light tanks, the other thirty-six being Type T-97 *Chi-Ha* medium tanks with their 57mm main guns. These would lead the attack, followed by 1,000 infantrymen of the 136th Infantry Regiment under Major Tirashi Hirakushi. It would be the largest Japanese tank attack of the war in the Pacific.

At 03.30 hours on 17 June, the Japanese launched their assault – and it was a disaster. Alerted to the impending attack by the rumbling of the tanks and the blowing of bugles, the 6th Marines were under arms as the enemy approached, disabling the tanks with their bazookas and 75mm guns. Twenty-nine of the Japanese tanks were destroyed, while some 700 of Hirakushi's men were cut down by the Marines' .50 calibre machine-guns. Shown here is one of the Type 97 tanks on fire. (NARA)

**Above:** Daylight on the 16th revealed the stark reality of the disastrous Japanese counter-attack. The horror of the scene was witnessed by Colonel Justice Chambers, 3rd Battalion, 25th Regiment, later on the 17th, as he was heading for a conference at regimental headquarters in his jeep. 'Somewhere along the way,' he recalled, 'we started running over dead bodies. As we rolled across them, they would burst. All of us were vomiting, and we had maybe 300 yards of bodies to go across. By the time we got back to the CP [Command Post], no one there would let us, or our jeep, anywhere near them.'[13] (USMC Archives)

Despite the relative success of D-Day, it would be six days before the beachhead was fully secured, with the Japanese displaying their usual tenacity. The next stage for Lieutenant General Holland M. Smith's men was to drive into the hills in the centre of Saipan where, painful experience had already shown, it could be certain that the enemy would withdraw to make its last stand.

The attack upon Mount Tipo Pale and Mount Tapochau began on 22 June, with, again, the Marines leading the way and the 27th Infantry Division in support, backed by eighteen artillery battalions. As expected, the advance was slow as the Marines, and, later in the day, the infantry, fought their way up steep ridges and down deep gullies, blasting the Japanese out of the caves that riddled the cliffs around Magicienne Bay.

On Mount Tapochau the Marines of the 4th Division were delayed in their advance because the infantry had failed to keep up, having encountered very stiff resistance and very rough terrain. Holland Smith saw this as being due to a lack of resolve on the part of the 27th Division's commander, Major General Ralph Smith, and he relieved him of his command. The following day,

**Above:** Displaying the M1A1 Bazooka with which they knocked out four Japanese light tanks are Pfc Lauren N. Kahn, left, and Pfc Lewis M. Nalder. The two Marines fired all their ammunition at Japanese tanks advancing in a counter-attack on the night of D+1. Kahn then grabbed some grenades, approached one tank from the side, and tossed the grenade into its open turret. Their action saved a 37mm gun crew, the objective of the tank. The gun crew, with its men wounded, was also out of ammunition. (Department of Defense)

25 June, the Marines seized Mount Tapochau, the highest point on the island. The 4th Marine Division also drove deeper into the Japanese positions on the Kagman Peninsula, and it was evident that all resistance there would soon be eliminated.

Slowly, day-by-day, one Japanese position after another in the hilly interior of Saipan was taken by the Marines and the 27th Division. On 29 June, near Garapan, the 2nd Marines were faced with the Japanese well dug-in on what was termed 'Flame Tree Hill', utilizing caves masked by the bright foliage on the slopes. That morning, these positions were pounded by artillery, mortars and machine-gun fire. As hoped, instead of sitting tight within the comparative safety of the dug-outs, the Japanese launched a counter-attack. As they left cover, the fire from the Marines intensified to such a degree that the attackers were wiped out almost to a man.

Though their tactics would evolve over the following months, the Japanese belief in the offensive over studied defence, led to massive and reckless loss of life. As we shall see, a week later this culminated in the largest Banzai charge of the war.

**Right:** On 16 June, the 105th and 165th regiments of the US Army's 27th Infantry Division landed on the beaches taken by the 4th Marine Division on D-Day, coming under the command of the Marines. The other regiment of the division, the 106th, was held back for possible deployment as reinforcements for the fighting on nearby Guam. (NARA)

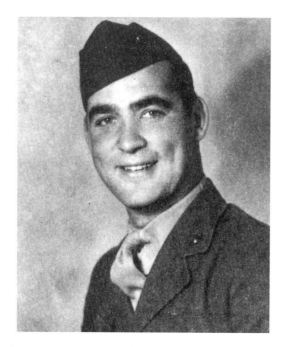

**Above:** Gunnery Sergeant Robert H. McCard USMC was posthumously awarded the Medal of Honor for his actions on 16 June. McCard was Platoon Sergeant of Company A, Fourth Tank Battalion, with the 4th Marine Division, when his tank was put out of action by a battery of Japanese 77mm guns. Cut off from the rest of his unit, McCard ordered his crew to escape while he diverted the enemy gunners' attention by standing up and throwing grenades at them. He was seriously wounded but continued to face the enemy until his supply of grenades ran out. He then dismantled one of the tank's machine-guns and fired at the battery, killing sixteen Japanese before he too was killed. (Department of Defense)

**Above:** With the Marines firmly established on Saipan, Holland Smith set up his headquarters ashore in this small house in Choran Kanos that had suffered only minor damage during the bombardment of the island. Here Smith is briefing some of his men. (USMC Archives)

**Below:** Aound midday on 17 June the 1st and 2nd battalions of the 165th Regiment launched an attack on Aslito airfield after a two-hour bombardment by American artillery. The Japanese response was, in their usual fashion, to counter-attack, which saw them lose heavily. Nevertheless, the 165th was forced to pull back and establish a defensive position of its own for the night. Here a number of Mitsubishi A6M Zeros are pictured on Aslito airfield after its capture. (USNHHC)

**Above:** The next morning the US troops renewed their assault on Aslito airfield, only to find that a large number of the Japanese had withdrawn to Nafutan Point and that the 43rd Division headquarters had re-established itself in the hills to the east of Garapan. This image shows another group of the Japanese aircraft captured at the airfield. (USNHHC)

**Below:** The Japanese aircraft on Guam that had survived the bombardment there made every effort to attack the US task force at sea off the islands. In this photograph, taken from USS *Coral Sea* (CVE-57), a Japanese plane crashes just astern of USS *Corregidor* (CVE-58) during an attack on 17 June. (US Navy)

**Above:** A Yokosuka Piyi 'Frances' medium bomber, burning from air attack hits, crosses the bow of USS *Corregidor* on 18 June as the Japanese aerial assault upon the task force continued. (USNHHC)

**Left:** On D+2, the 2nd Marines continued its advance towards Garapan, reaching positions within 1,000 yards of Saipan's main town. In this photograph a 37mm light field gun fires on Japanese positions near Garapan. The original caption states that 'what appears to be peep holes in the gun shield, are bullet holes from enemy fire'. (USMC Archives)

**Right:** At their 20mm anti-aircraft guns, crewmen on the aircraft carrier USS *Kitkun Bay* (CVE-71) watch as Japanese plane crashes in flames during an air attack off Saipan on 18 June. (USNHHC)

**Above:** A Japanese plane is shot down during a dusk attack on Task Group 52.11 off Saipan on 18 June as seen from USS *Coral Sea*, with USS *Corregidor* in the background. (USNHHC)

**Left:** A Japanese twin-engine aircraft is shot down while attacking escort carriers of Task Group 52.11 off Saipan on 18 June. This is another photograph taken from USS *Kitkun Bay*. A pair of Grumman TBM-1C Avengers can be seen on the flight deck in the foreground. (US Navy)

**Below:** Smaller craft follow the command ship USS *Rocky Mount* as it shifts anchorage at Saipan on 18 June. (USNHHC)

# SAIPAN 1944

**Main image:** It was shortly before midnight on 18 June that Admiral Nimitz radioed Spruance to inform him that a message had been intercepted from the Japanese 1st Mobile Fleet, which was at that point less than 400 miles from Task Force 58. While Spruance and Mitscher turned their attention towards Vice-Admiral Jisaburō Ozawa's approaching warships, operations continued ashore.

Consequently, on 19 June those warships that had remained off Saipan began a preliminary bombardment of Garapan in advance of the assault upon the city by the 2nd Marines. Note the destroyer offshore on the left of the picture, taken as the naval and marine shells burst in the town. (USNHHC)

**Right:** On 19 June, the 165th Regiment and elements of the 4th Marine Division reached Magicienne Bay on Saipan's eastern coast. In doing so they effectively isolated the southern part of the island. By this time Saitō, after his failed counter-attacks, knew that he had to adopt a defensive stance. He concentrated the bulk of his remaining forces on the approaches to Mount Tapochau, effectively leaving his troops in the southern part of the island below Garapan to fight on alone as best they could. He relayed this battle plan to Tokyo: 'The Army is consolidating its battle lines and has decided to prepare for a showdown fight. It is concentrating the 43rd Division in the area east of Tapochau. The remaining units (including naval forces) are concentrating in the area east of Garapan.'[14] This image shows an early production Willys Jeep, heavily field-modified into a litter Jeep, carrying wounded soldiers and medics on Saipan. (United States Army Signal Corps)

**Below:** The seaplane tender USS *Onslow* (AVP-48) is pictured here off Saipan on 22 June whilst operating in support of the attack upon the central mountain range. The photograph was taken from USS *Pocomoke*. (US Navy)

**Right:** The attack upon Saipan's central mountain chain began at 06.00 hours on 22 June (D+7). Holland Smith's original plan to capture the heights involved an advance by the 2nd Marine Division up the western edge of the hills while the 4th Division moved up the eastern side from Magicienne Bay. But both divisions had suffered heavy losses (the 2nd Division 2,514 casualties and the 4th Division 3,628) and so Smith ordered Ralph Smith's 27th Infantry Division to join the advance, taking up a central position. As Marine General Harry Schmidt's 4th Division moved up the east coast, it encountered a succession of deep gullies interspersed with rough, rocky outcrops from the top of which the enemy could pour fire upon the exposed attackers. In this image, a Marine has thrown a hand grenade at an enemy position, whilst a second Marine is about to throw his grenade, the fuze on which is already burning. (USNHHC)

**Above:** Bombs burst nearby as USS *Manila Bay* (CVE-61) comes under attack by four Zeros off Saipan at 12.05 hours on 23 June. Note the USAAF P-47s on the flight deck, intended for delivery to Aslito airfield. (USNHHC)

**Above:** As the Marines and infantry moved deeper into the northern hills, they encountered a number of rocky heights that would soon be christened with chilling names that reflected the nature of the struggle the men faced – names such as 'Death Valley', 'Hell's Gate' and 'Purple Heart Ridge'.

The challenges that these areas represented was well described by Colonel Albert K. Stebbins Jr., the 27th Division's chief of staff: 'The cliffs and hillsides were pocketed with small caves and large caves. The wooded area was rough, filled with boulders, and excellent for defensive operations. Bands of fire were laid by the enemy thru the underbrush and in such manner as to make it most difficult to discover their locations. Well-placed, hostile guns fired only when lines passed and striking our forces in the rear disrupted the attack.'

Though the infantry was supported by the 762nd Tank Battalion, the men spent the afternoon inching their way along the valley as the Japanese fired down on them from Mount Tapochau and the opposing ridgeline. The tanks were so severely battered by artillery fire from these two elevated positions that by sunset only eighteen of the seventy-two which had started the battle were still functioning. (NARA)

**Above:** On Mount Tapochau the Marines of the 4th Division were delayed in their advance because the infantry had failed to keep up with them, having encountered very stiff resistance and very rough terrain as they struggled to overcome the Japanese positions on Purple Heart Ridge. Holland Smith saw this as being due to a lack of resolve on the part of the 27th Division's commander Ralph Smith, as a member of Holland Smith's staff told a correspondent of *Time* magazine: 'We cannot attack M. Tapochau until the 27th Division moves up, and we've got to have the high ground so we can look down the Japs' throats instead of letting them look down ours. If we don't keep pressing them, they'll reorganise and dig in deeper, and casualties will shoot up higher. We can't sit back and expect artillery and naval gunfire to blast them out of the caves.'[15] In what would prove to be a highly contentious move, which would sour relations between the Army and the Marines for many months to come, Holland Smith, who had not visited the front line, concluded that the 27th Division's disappointing progress was because its commander lacked the necessary drive. Though he had made his mind up to relieve Ralph Smith of his command, Holland Smith decided to give the 27th Division one more day to try and catch up. (NARA)

**Left:** Unknown to Holland Smith, Saitō had concentrated his strongest force to cover Death Valley. This consisted of his most complete infantry regiment, the 135th, as well as a number of headquarters units and all his remaining armoured vehicles; in all, a total of around 4,000 men. These troops occupied almost every cave on the eastern side of Mount Tapochau and the western side of Purple Heart Ridge. The Army tried to push on and take these Japanese positions, but casualties reached frightening proportions, the fighting eventually resulting in the loss of twenty-two out of the 165th Infantry Regiment's company commanders. Heavy fire kept the US troops pinned down and no further progress was made that day, 24 June. But, by that time, Ralph Smith was no longer in command of the 27th Division.

Here a USMC M3A1 flamethrower light tank is pictured in action against Japanese positions during the fighting on Saipan. (USMC Archives)

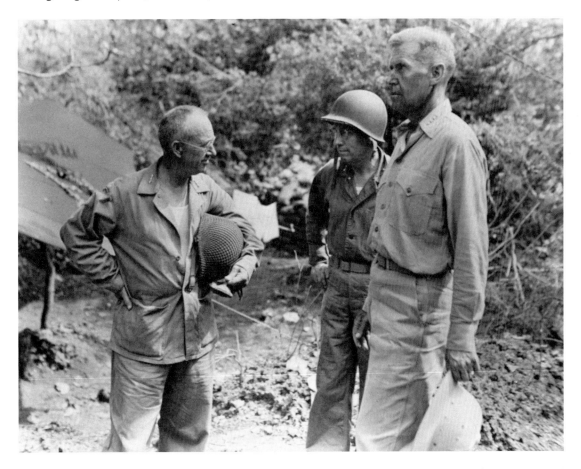

**Above:** In relieving Ralph Smith of his command, Holland Smith said: 'Ralph Smith's my friend, but good God, I've got a duty to my country. I've lost seven thousand Marines. Can I afford to lose back what they have gained? To let my Marines die in vain? I know I am sticking my neck out … but my conscience is clear. I did my duty. When Ralph Smith issued an order to hold after I had told him to attack, I had no other choice than to relieve him.'[16] Here we see Holland Smith, on the left holding his helmet, discussing the tactical situation on Saipan with Major General Thomas E. Watson, the Commanding General of the 2nd Marine Division, and Admiral Spruance, at the 2nd Division's headquarters. (USNHHC)

**Left:** The man handed command of the 27th Division, albeit only temporarily, was Major General Sanderford Jarman, who had been designated commander of the Saipan garrison after its capture. He agreed to implement a new plan of attack that Ralph Smith had devised before his departure, in which the 165th Regiment would pin down the enemy with a frontal assault while the 106th Regiment moved eastwards and then swung round to the north to outflank the Purple Heart Ridge. However, the 106th came upon the Japanese 31st Army headquarters in a strong position supported by artillery and the 165th found itself tied down at the entrance to Death Valley by 'murderous' crossfire from the ridges above.

The Marines, on the other hand, progressed well on the 25th. The 8th and 29th Marine regiments, for their part, closed in upon the summit of Mount Tapochau, while the men of the 4th Marine Division also drove deeper into the Japanese positions on the Kagman Peninsula. It was evident that all resistance in the latter part of Saipan would soon be eliminated.

In this photograph a US Marine is pictured employing his flamethrower to neutralise the threat from a cave hidden behind a house in what was originally known as Paradise Valley, but which the Japanese called the 'Valley of Hell'.[17] (USMC Archives)

**Below:** The same cave pictured after any threat that it and its occupants presented had been dealt with by the Marines. (Library of Congress)

**Above:** During their advance through Saipan, the Marines and infantrymen encountered a number of dummy positions constructed by the Japanese – such as this fake searchlight. (USMC Archives)

**Right:** Marine First Sergeant Neil I. Shober 'shares the spoils of war – bananas – with a native goat, one of the few survivors of the terrific naval and air bombardment in support of the Marines hitting the beach'. (USMC Archives)

**Below:** The capture of Aslito airfield gave the Americans the advantage of being able to support their ground forces more closely. In this photograph USAAF P-47 fighters of the 73rd Fighter Squadron, 7th Air Force, are being launched from USS *Manila Bay* for delivery to Aslito airfield on 24 June. (USNHHC)

**Above:** A wrecked tank acts as an altar during the fighting on Saipan. Although this photograph is said to have been taken on 24 June, it was most likely the following day, the 25th, as this was a Sunday. (USMC Archives)

**Top right:** The rusting remains of a US M5A1 Stuart tank of the 4th Marine Division. It was knocked out by Japanese anti-tank fire during the fighting on the Kagman Peninsula on 25 June. The wreck was discovered during excavation work undertaken as part of the construction of the LaoLao Bay Golf Resort on Saipan. (John Grehan Collection)

**Bottom right:** Two P-47 fighters 'buzz' the Casablanca-class escort carrier USS *Natoma Bay* (CVE-62) after taking off for Saipan, where they will be based, on 23 June. After loading thirty-seven P-47s of the 7th Air Force, *Natoma Bay* had departed Pearl Harbor on 5 June, en route to the Marianas. Steaming via Eniwetok, she arrived off Saipan on 19 June, initially being ordered to retire eastward. On the 22nd she steamed westward and commenced despatching the USAAF aircraft to Aslito airfield. A total of twenty-five took off on the 22nd, the remainder early on the 23rd. Following this, *Natoma Bay* then headed to a refuelling area some forty-five miles east of Saipan. (USNHHC)

**Above:** Men of the 4th Marine Division rest in 'a burned-out cane field, near a former Jap observation post' on 25 June. This is, continues the original captian, 'a Marine patrol which has been scouting the eastern coast of Saipan'. (NARA)

**Below:** Marines advancing up a hill during their advance on Saipan. (NARA)

**Left:** In the early hours of 25 June, the Japanese launched a counter-attack, targeting positions held by the 1st Battalion, 6th Marines. Private First Class Harold Epperson, manning a machine-gun emplacement, found himself facing the brunt of the 'fanatical' attack.

The subsequent citation for Epperson's award of a posthumous Medal of Honor notes that he opened fire, 'with determined aggressiveness, fighting furiously in the defense of his battalion's position and maintaining a steady stream of devastating fire against rapidly infiltrating hostile troops to aid materially in annihilating several of the enemy and in breaking the abortive attack. Suddenly a Japanese soldier, assumed to be dead, sprang up and hurled a powerful hand grenade into the emplacement. Determined to save his comrades, Pfc. Epperson unhesitatingly chose to sacrifice himself and, diving upon the deadly missile, absorbed the shattering violence of the exploding charge in his own body. Stout hearted and indomitable in the face of certain death, Pfc. Epperson fearlessly yielded his own life that his able comrades might carry on the relentless battle against a ruthless enemy.' Thanks to Epperson's courage the attack was beaten off.

The Medal of Honor was presented to Epperson's mother in a ceremony held in a stadium in the town where he grew up on 4 July 1945. Some 8,500 people came to honour him. (Department of Defense)

**Below:** Reinforcements being brought ashore on Saipan on 26 June. (NARA)

**Below:** Progress on Saipan continued to be tough and slow. Here Marines take a break from the fighting by a camouflaged 75mm pack howitzer emplacement. One of those involved in the battle, Private Rod Sandburg, told of the conditions the men operated in: 'We ate, slept, and fought in clothes that became so rotten from perspiration and rain that they were very threadbare when the campaign were over … our dungarees would rot from body sweat, right on our bodies.'[18] (USNHHC)

**Right:** As June drew to a close, Saitō was increasingly aware that defeat on Saipan was inevitable. He subsequently sent the following message to Tokyo: 'Please apologise deeply to the Emperor that we cannot do better than we are doing … There is no hope for victory in places where we do not have control of the air and we are still hoping here for aerial reinforcements … Praying for the good health of the Emperor, we all cry "Banzai!".'[19] Nevertheless, what Japanese aircraft remained operational in the area still tried to inflict damage on the task force and in this photograph a bomb near misses USS *Wasp*, as seen from USS *Monterey* (CVL-26), off Saipan on 26 June. (USNHHC)

**Above:** The port side and after 5-inch/38 guns of USS *Wichita* firing on Japanese positions on Saipan on 26 June in support of the ongoing operations on the island. The guns' simultaneous discharge indicates they are firing under director control. (USNHHC)

**Right:** American troops examine recently captured Japanese positions on 26 June, as the bitterly contested US advance towards the north of Saipan continued. Colonel Stebbins of the 106th Infantry, for example, described how his men fought their way through Death Valley: 'It was necessary to work forward taking out each gun in turn, employing tanks to draw fire so that guns could be located and destroyed. Rush and die tactics would never have succeeded.'[20] (Department of Defense)

**Above:** A 20-year-old Private First Class in Company E, 2nd Battalion, 23rd Marines, Robert F. Graf, described how the Marines dealt with the Japanese ensconced in the caves: 'The firepower was intense, and we were working our way up to where the shots originated. Quite often there would be multi cave openings, each protecting another. Laying down heavy cover fire, our specialist would advance to near the mouth of the cave.

'A satchel charge would then be heaved into the mouth of the cave, followed by a loud blast as the dynamite exploded. Other times it might be grenades thrown inside the cave, both fragment type, which exploded sending bits of metal all throughout the cave, and other times phosphorous grenades that burned the enemy. Also the flame thrower was used, sending a sheet of flame into the cave, burning anyone that was in its path. Screams could be heard and on occasions the enemy would emerge from the caves, near the entrance, we would call upon the tanks, and these monsters would get in real close and pump shells into the opening.'[21]

A number of the caves were very strongly constructed or impressive in scale. A fellow rifleman from Graf's company told him this story: 'You should go up and see the huge cave that I was just in. It was

large and contained a completely equipped operating room, all the medical equipment, surgical tools, etc. The tools were made from German surgical steel.'[22] Just such a well-constructed cave, and seemingly well-stocked cave, is shown in this photograph being examined by US personnel after its capture. (USMC Archives)

**Above:** As the American advance rolled onwards – during when this picture of Marines in action supported by an LVT was taken – Saitō knew that he could not hold back the Americans much longer. Though the Marines and infantrymen had often battled hard for the territory they captured, they had also taken a heavy toll on the Japanese holding Purple Heart Ridge, with 3,000 out of the 4,000 men defending that area becoming casualties. General Jarman's tenure in command of the 27th Division came to an end on 27 June when Holland Smith handed the job to Major General George Grinder. Fortunately for Grinder, the Marines on both his flanks continued to make progress with Saitō's men being squeezed into an ever-smaller area. The Japanese commander decided to make his last stand in the north in the area between Tanapag Harbour and Marpi Point. (NARA)

**Top left:** Further south, the 8th Marines had been handed the task of taking Garapan, but the Japanese in the south had made a stand at the southern extremity of the island at Nafutan Point. It was only when these had been eliminated that the assault upon Garapan could begin. This image, taken a little later on 2 July, shows a captured 6-inch gun at Nafutan Point. (National Museum of the US Navy)

**Bottom left:** The task of taking Nafutan Point was handed to the 2nd Battalion, 105th Infantry Regiment. The attack did not begin until 13.30 hours on 23 June and little was achieved. As with the troops in the north, the Japanese ensconced themselves in the caves which honeycombed the cliffs and the infantrymen had to fight for every few years of ground they seized, as the battalion's narrative explained: 'Enemy resistance on the ridges was stubborn. The terrain consisted of steep ridges, deep gulches with cliffs, ground broken with coral pinnacles and thick jungles type underbrush which impeded progress and made observation impossible.'[23]

To help the infantry, the navy destroyers pounded the rocks and caves unmercifully. The result of this shelling can be seen here in this painting of a shore battery near Nafutan Point by Robert Benney. The battery was destroyed by the naval guns. The gun represented in this scene was captured by the Japanese at British Samoa and moved to Saipan. (USNHHC)

**Below:** A Japanese gun emplacement at Nafutan Point photographed after its capture. During the final stages of the fighting in this area, Captain Sasaki, who commanded the force of defenders at Nafutan Point, the 317th Independent Infantry Battalion of the 47th Independent Mixed Brigade, decided to break out on the night of 26/27 June, aiming for Aslito airfield and a nearby hill – Hill 500. Unfortunately for Sasaki's men, they crashed into the 14th Marine Artillery and 25th Marine Regiment and approximately 500 Japanese were killed. (USNHHC)

**Above:** The 2nd Marines moved into the outskirts of Garapan on the morning of 25 June. The streets of Saipan's capital were choked with piles of rubble, tin roofing, chunks of concrete, and charred timbers from the bombing and shelling. Some of the streets had been mined with converted aerial bombs and snipers waited for the unwary. This photograph shows a group of US Marines advancing understandably cautiously towards Garapan. (Library of Congress)

**Top right:** A group of Marines pictured in a foxhole near the front line in Saipan on 1 July, presumably waiting for the main assault upon Garapan to begin. On the night of 28 June, Saitō instructed his troops to evacuate Garapan and join him in the north of the island for his symbolic last stand. As the Japanese

troops tried to withdraw, they encountered the advancing 2nd Marines and a fierce battle ensued in the rubble-strewn streets.

Private Guy Gabaldon, who was with the Intelligence Unit of the 2nd Marines, was among the first into the ruined capital: 'The town had been thoroughly bombed and strafed, but our observation posts had reported seeing Japs milling in and around the buildings. We approached a well-built concrete building in South Garapan and started crawling. I went toward the west end and Johnny right toward the east end of the building. Suddenly, two Japanese soldiers came out of the building and stood at the door … I fired off fifteen rounds, point blank. They were so close that it wasn't necessary to aim. I emptied the clip right from the hip. They both fell down, one down the steps onto the grass, the other on the concrete deck.'[24] (Library of Congress)

**Left:** Marines of the 2nd Marine Division use a captured Japanese tank to bombard enemy positions on Saipan. With the threat from the Japanese on Nafutan Point largely negated, the final push towards Garapan could take place.

On 29 June, near Garapan, the 2nd Marines were faced with the Japanese well dug-in on what was termed 'Flame Tree Hill', utilizing caves masked by the bright foliage on the hill. That morning, these positions were pounded by artillery, mortars and machine-gun fire. As hoped, instead of sitting tight within the comparative safety of the dug-outs, the Japanese launched a counter-attack. As they left cover, the fire from the Marines was intensified and the attacking force was wiped out almost to a man. (USMC Archive)

**Above:** Pictured during the attack on Garapan, this group of Marines are firing on Japanese positions with a captured Type 92 battalion gun or light howitzer. (NARA)

**Below:** Japanese-held buildings and positions in Garapan continued to be attacked from the air. Here a Martin PBM Mariner flying boat of VP-16 takes off for patrol duty in Saipan roadstead on 30 June. (USNHHC)

**Right:** Smoke rises from a huge oil dump fire on Mutcho Point, Garapan, after an air strike on 30 June, as seen from USS *Pocomoke*, with the seaplane tender USS *Chandeleur* (AV-10) in the foreground. (USNHHC)

**Above:** As the noose tightens around the Japanese garrison in Garapan, a 105mm howitzer is pictured firing on Saipan's capital on 1 July. Following the battle for Saipan, Holland Smith himself later declared that, 'never before in the Pacific had Marines gone into action with so much armament, ranging from 75s to 155s'. (USMC Archives)

**Opposite page:** Pfc Carl Gorman, described in the original caption as an 'Indian Marine', mans an observation post on a hill overlooking Garapan as preparations for the final assault on Saipan's capital are completed.

At 22.45 hours on 1 July, the 2nd Marines received attack orders to begin the advance. The next morning, at 10.30 hours, the first of the attackers moved out. The 8th Marines, having exchanged places with the 2nd Marines, attacked with the 1st Battalion, ahead of the 3rd Battalion which was held in reserve. Colonel Stuart's men made excellent progress.

The days and weeks of pounding from the US Navy paid dividends. Supported by Company C of the 2nd Tank Battalion, the 3rd Marines swept through the rubble-strewn streets at a steady pace. Encountering rifle and machine-gun fire, the men took advantage of the protection afforded by the torn hunks of rubble littering the area. With tanks ricocheting rounds among the shattered ruins, the Marines moved into the very heart of what had once been Saipan's largest town. (NARA)

**Right:** A destroyed street in Garapan pictured on 2 July 1944. By 12.00 hours that day, the 3rd Battalion, supported by Company C, 2nd Tank Battalion, was 800 yards inside the town, 'finding grim evidence of what artillery, aircraft, and naval guns could do'. (USMC Archives)

**Above:** The battered shell of a Japanese shop in Garapan – again pictured on 2 July. As one account notes: 'Japanese soldiers were still there – not many, but some – and hostile fire was encountered. Some American war correspondents reported that at Garapan the Marines experienced their first street fighting of World War II. According to division accounts, however, "actually there was little, if any, of this type of fighting compared to European standards. ... The town had been leveled completely".'[25] (USMC Archives)

**Left:** A Japanese field gun seized during the capture of Garapan, pictured on 2 July. The original caption notes that the 'piece [was] aimed toward the waterfront'.

One official history details how this gun might have been dealt with: 'Twisted metal roof tops now littered the area [in Garapan], shielding Japanese snipers. A number of deftly-hidden pillboxes were scattered among the ruins. Assault engineers, covered by riflemen, slipped behind such obstacles to set explosives while flamethrowers seared the front. Assisted by the engineers, and supported by tanks and 75mm self-propelled guns of the Regimental Weapons Company, the 2d Marines beat down the scattered resistance before nightfall. On the beaches, suppressing fire from the LVT(A)s of the 2d Armored Amphibian Battalion silenced Japanese weapons located near the water.'[26] (USMC Archives)

**Above:** A fuel dump burns as US personnel complete the capture of Garapan. Note the church steeple in the foreground. (USMC Archives)

**111**

**Top left:** Marines engaged in house to house fighting in Garapan on the final day of the battle for the town, 3 July, as the last pocket of resistance in the city was finally eliminated. (National Museum of the US Navy)

**Bottom left:** Destroyed Japanese seaplanes and vehicles, including the mobile searchlight in the foreground, pictured at Mutcho Point on 8 July 1944. Having eliminated a small Japanese garrison, Mutcho Point was captured by the men of the 3rd Battalion, 2nd Marines early on the morning of 4 July.

As one account notes, 'The only headache of the operation was an enemy heavy antiaircraft gun farther up the shore, which delivered air bursts uncomfortably close to the attacking troops'. (National Museum of the US Navy)

**Above:** The scale of the destruction wrought on Garapan during the fighting in June and July 1944 is evident in this aerial photograph taken soon after the city's capture. (National Museum of the US Navy)

**Above:** With Garapan and the southern part of Saipan secure, battle-weary Marines march back from the front on 5 July. But Saitō was still holding out in the far north of the island and there was still much blood to be shed before Saipan was secure. (USMC Archives)

Chapter 5

# THE BATTLE OF THE PHILIPPINE SEA

19-20 June 1944

**Above:** US submarines had been searching for the Japanese fleet, which had been divided into two groups – A Force and B Force – behind a powerful vanguard which included four battleships and eight heavy cruisers, and at 04.00 hours on 18 June, Admiral Mitscher was informed that the USS *Cavalla* had detected one of the enemy groups. This picture shows Lieutenant Commander Herman J. Kossler, *Cavalla*'s captain, being interviewed in June 1944 – presumably after the Battle of the Philippine Sea.

From the information received from Kossler, it was calculated that Ozawa would be 660 miles west of Saipan at dawn. If Task Force 58 immediately began moving toward the Japanese force, Ozawa's First Mobile Fleet would be within range of US carrier aircraft by late afternoon.

While the fighting raged on Saipan, the largest carrier-to-carrier battle in history was being fought in the Philippine Sea.

As early as 14 June 1944, the Pacific Fleet intelligence officer, Commander Edwin Layton, advised Admiral Nimitz that the Japanese were intent on disrupting Operation *Forager*. The Imperial High Command was acutely aware of the importance of the Marianas and every effort was to be made to save Saipan. Under Operation *A-Go*, there was also a hope that Task Force 58 could be taken by surprise and destroyed – and in so doing re-establish Japan's naval superiority in the Pacific.

It was a vain hope. Washington was able to read Japan's secret signals and Vice-Admiral Marc A. Mitscher's Fast Carrier Task Force of seven fleet and eight light carriers with more than 900 fighters, torpedo-bombers and dive bombers, would be ready and waiting for the Japanese to approach within striking distance.

Aircraft from seven carriers of the US Fifth Fleet and five from the Japanese Mobile Fleet met shortly after 10.00 hours on 19 June. The first wave of fifty Japanese aircraft from Guam was intercepted by Grumman F6F Hellcats, with thirty-five of the enemy being destroyed by the superior American aircraft.

The next attack was delivered by almost seventy aircraft from the Japanese carriers, but not one of them got through to the US carriers. The following wave was even greater, consisting of 107 aircraft. Though a few bombers did reach the US carriers, they were unable to inflict more than minor damage, and the penalty the attackers paid was to see all but ten of their machines destroyed. The next Japanese attack was delivered by just forty-seven aircraft. This time, when the US fighters were encountered, not all the Japanese pilots pressed home their attack and only seven were brought down.

A final attempt was made by the Japanese to hit the US ships, but they failed to locate the carrier group. They divided into two groups to return to Guam and the smaller island of Rota, but were once again pounced on by Hellcats and all forty-nine were destroyed. One pilot from the USS *Lexington* was heard to remark that the fighting that day was like 'an old-time turkey shoot', and the epithet was thereafter used to describe the Battle of the Philippine Sea.[27]

Whilst its aircraft had failed to locate the Japanese fleet, the US Navy's submarines had more success. The USS *Albacore*, for example, sank the carrier *Taihō*, whilst a torpedo from the USS *Cavalla* (SS-244) resulted in a catastrophic explosion aboard the carrier *Shōkaku* which blew the ship apart.

The next day, 20 June, further patrols were flown from the US carriers in an effort to try and find the enemy fleet, and it was almost 16.00 hours before it was believed that a positive sighting was made. But, after the first wave of aircraft had taken off, it was discovered that the Japanese ships were, in reality, sixty miles further away. This meant the enemy was at the absolute limit of the range of the Hellcat fighters and Grumman Avenger torpedo-bombers and that it would be dark before they could return to the carriers. A second attack wave was therefore cancelled.

Those that carried on in the first wave, sunk the fleet carrier *Hiyō* and damaged three others. The only negative aspect of this raid was that some of the returning aircraft ran out of fuel and others crashed onto the flight decks as they landed in the dark. Eighty aircraft were lost.

However, the Japanese carrier fleet, along with its irreplaceable pilots and planes, had been irrevocably wrecked. There was no Japanese naval force left to oppose the US warships; the Pacific was thereafter controlled by the Allied fleets. This meant that the US, along with the Royal Navy and the navies of Australia and New Zealand, could concentrate their respective strengths against any Japanese territory without the threat of any serious intervention from the Imperial Japanese Navy. Complete control of the vast expanse of the Pacific Ocean was finally in Allied hands.

**Above:** For Operation *A-Go*, the 'decisive' battle that the Japanese had sought since Pearl Harbor, the Imperial Japanese Navy would commit sixty-nine warships under the command of Vice-Admiral Jisaburō Ozawa's First Mobile Fleet. These included five fleet carriers, four light carriers, five battleships, eleven heavy cruisers, two light cruisers, and twenty-three destroyers, supported by nineteen submarines. His carriers embarked half the number of aircraft on the US carriers, but he could count on a further 300 aircraft from the airfields on Rota and Guam. The Japanese carrier aircraft could also make use of those airfields, which would allow them to launch at distance, have their aircraft attack the US fleet and then land on the island airfields. They then could shuttle back to the carriers and attack again on the return flight. The scene was set, therefore, for the largest carrier-to-carrier battle the world had ever seen.

The importance of the battle was made clear to Ozawa, seen here, by Admiral Soemu Toyoda, Commander-in-Chief of the Combined Fleet, on 15 June 1944: 'The rise and fall of Imperial Japan depends on this one battle. Every man shall do his utmost.' The instructions that Ozawa received were unambiguous: 'Attack the enemy in the Marianas area and annihilate his fleet'[28]. (USNHHC)

THE BATTLE OF THE PHILIPPINE SEA

**Top left:** Ozawa, on the other hand, believed that Spruance would keep his carriers within 100 to 200 miles of Saipan in order to ensure the landings were not exposed to an attack. Consequently, Ozawa planned to keep his forces outside the maximum range of US carrier aircraft and then use his range advantage to hit the American carriers. This photograph is of the battleship *Yamato* which formed part of the First Mobile Fleet's vanguard.

The Yamato-class battleships carried the largest ordnance – 18-inch guns – and were the heaviest battleships ever constructed. (Kure Maritime Museum)

**Bottom left:** At daybreak on the 18th, both sides despatched scout planes to seek out their respective enemies, but without success. But that evening Ozawa made a terrible mistake by transmitting a radio message to Vice-Admiral Kakuji Kakuta who, based on Tinian, was commander of the remaining Japanese land-based aircraft in the Marianas. His message was picked up by the Pacific Fleet's high frequency direction finding (HFDF) network which duly obtained an accurate fix on Ozawa's position. Needless to say this was quickly disseminated to Spruance.

Mitscher requested permission to launch a night attack on the Japanese fleet, but Spruance acted with great caution, wishing to have a visual sighting of the enemy before releasing the aircraft. Before dawn, both sides launched search aircraft again. Though there were aerial contacts, with the Japanese in particular losing aircraft, there were no sightings of any ships until 07.30 hours, when an Aichi E13A floatplane, such as the one shown here, spotted two US carriers.

Further reports were received. Ozawa turned south to preserve distance and ordered his strike aircraft to commence launching. Unknown to Ozawa, Spruance's aircraft had taken a heavy toll of the Japanese planes on Guam and the shore-based squadrons were unable to make any significant impact on the battle that was about to unfold. (USNHHC)

**Right:** By the morning of the 19th, Mitscher had formed the tasks groups under his command into two lines and, like Ozawa, had placed battleships ahead to deliver a powerful anti-aircraft barrage at the oncoming enemy. Their gunfire would soon be tested as, between 08.30 and 11.30 hours, Ozawa's nine carriers would launch 326 aircraft in four raids, almost as many as the attack on Pearl Harbor.

But unlike that raid which had opened the war in the Pacific, the attackers would encounter literally hundreds of Hellcats – in fact more than 450 of them – and the Japanese aircraft would find themselves utterly outclassed.

This image depicts a Hellcat from USS *Essex* which had a full squadron of around forty of these fighters embarked, as well as between fifty and sixty Curtiss SB2C Helldiver dive bombers and Avenger torpedo bombers. (US Navy)

**Left:** Remarkably, such was the ability of radio intelligence teams to intercept Japanese signals, they were able to tune into Japanese radio operators making pre-flight checks, which were then confirmed by additional in-flight checks. The radio intelligence team could even make rough estimates of the rate of closure based on signal strength. Consequently, Mitscher had warning of the Japanese raids before they had even taken off! Here a Hellcat is towed to the next position prior to launching from Mitscher's flag ship USS *Lexington* with Task Group 58.3. (USNHHC)

**Above:** The Hellcats were launched into the sky to ambush the Japanese aircraft when the enemy were seventy-two miles from *Lexington*. Lieutenant Commander C.W. Brewster was the first to engage the enemy aircraft, shooting down two bombers and two of the escorting Zero fighters. Soon the other Hellcat squadrons joined the fray. Vapour trails left by the American fighters during the Japanese air attack on 19 June can be seen in this photograph taken from *Lexington*. (USNHHC)

**Above:** A Japanese plane shot down while attacking Task Group 58.3 on 19 June can just be seen, to the right, falling in flames. It is the USS *Enterprise* that is on the left. Of the sixty-nine Japanese aircraft deployed in this first attack, forty-two were destroyed. (USNHHC)

**Top right:** With their aircraft launched, the flight deck crew of one of the US carriers can only act as observers as the battle rages in the sky around them. The original caption states that these vapour trails were produced by the Hellcats of Task Group 58.2, which was commanded by Rear Admiral Alfred E. Montgomery who was embarked on USS *Bunker Hill* (CV-17). (US Navy)

**Bottom right:** One of the attacking Japanese aircraft disintegrates in the air during the strike on Task Group 58.2, as seen from USS *Monterey*. (USNHHC)

**Overleaf:** A Japanese bomb explodes close alongside USS *Bunker Hill* in the opening phases of the action on 19 June. In this attack 119 Japanese aircraft that reached the target area were engaged by 162 Hellcats, which claimed eighty shot down. Another six to eight were reported to have been downed by anti-aircraft fire. Only twenty-three made it back to the Japanese carriers and eight to Guam. (USNHHC)

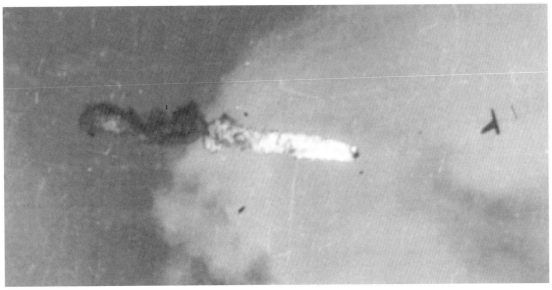

**Above:** A third, and then fourth, raids were undertaken by the Japanese with forty-seven and eighty-four aircraft respectively. Of the third group, a few Japanese machines got past the Hellcats and one dropped a bomb close to USS *Essex*. The fourth raid was ordered to target the American carriers, land on Guam, re-arm, refuel, and strike again on the way back to their carriers. However, they failed to find the US carriers and they split up, with twenty returning back to the Shōkaku-class carrier *Zuikaku* and the rest heading for Guam. These, though, were intercepted by *Essex*'s Hellcats. Thirty were shot down and a further nineteen which reached Guam were too badly shot up to be of any further use. This is a photograph of Mitscher watching the action on 19 June from USS *Lexington*. (National Museum of the US Navy)

**Top right:** Heavy anti-aircraft fire from ships of Task Group 58.3 claims one of the Japanese attackers, which falls into the sea – marked by the small splash in the centre of the view. The picture was taken from USS *Enterprise*. (USNHHC)

**Bottom right:** USS *Bunker Hill* sustained a near-miss from a Japanese bomb during the attacks on 19 June. The Japanese aircraft, with its tail shot off, is about to crash on the left. In fact, three bombs exploded in the general vicinity of *Bunker Hill* without causing any damage. During evasive action, as the carrier turned at high speed, a Hellcat was thrown over the side with the pilot still in it. He was rescued. This photograph was taken from USS *Monterey*. (USNHHC)

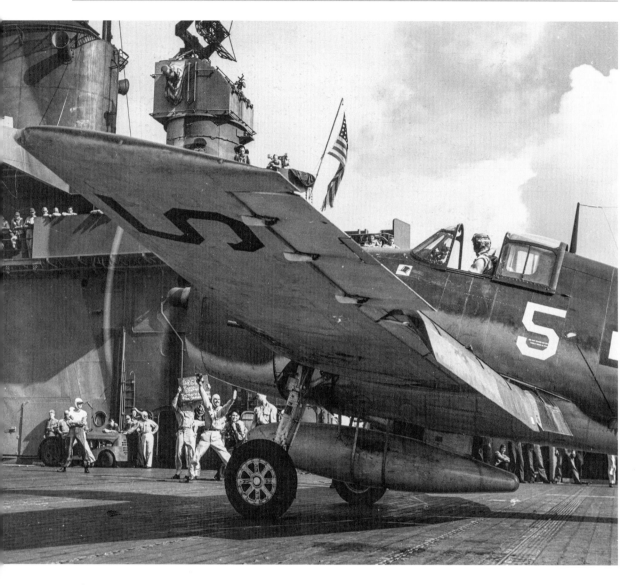

**Above:** A Hellcat is launched from USS *Yorktown* (CV-10) to intercept enemy forces during the fighting on 19 June. Note the target information board on the carrier's island behind the aircraft's propeller. (USNHHC)

**Top right:** An F6F-3 Hellcat fighter lands back on USS *Lexington* on 19 June 1944. Note the 40mm guns in the foreground, and 20mm guns along the starboard side of the carrier's flight deck. (USNHHC)

**Bottom right:** A US Navy submarine gets underway after having rescued a downed aviator, off Saipan, on 19 June. The photograph was taken by an aircraft operating from USS *Lexington*. (USNHHC)

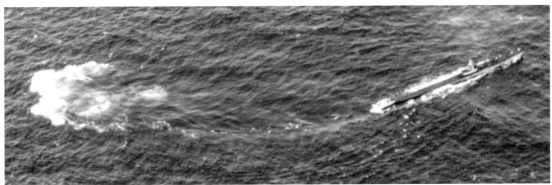

**Left:** Pictured on the flight deck of USS *Lexington*, Lieutenant Junior Grade Alexander Vraciu USNR holds up six fingers to signify his 'kills' during the 'Great Marianas Turkey Shoot' on 19 June 1944. Vraciu was initially nominated for a Medal of Honor for the six victories, but the recommendation was eventually accepted as a Navy Cross. (USNHHC)

**Above:** The Japanese fleet was also under attack, but from below the waves not above them. The submarine USS *Albacore*, which had been directed towards the Japanese ships through the intelligence gathered from communication intercepts, came upon the enemy carriers. Sighting the carriers, Commander James W. Blanchard managed to fire all six forward tubes before diving as Japanese destroyers bore down on his command. One of those six torpedoes found its mark, hitting the carrier *Taihō*. There would have been a second hit except that Warrant Officer Sakio Komatsu, who had just launched in a Nakajima B6N Tenzan torpedo bomber, sighted the torpedo and deliberately flew his plane into the water and detonated the torpedo, sacrificing his and his gunner's lives to save his ship.[29]

    *Albacore*'s first torpedo hit *Taihō* on the starboard side but did not at first appear to have seriously damaged the carrier, which resumed operations thirty minutes later. However, at 15.30 hours a massive explosion wracked the carrier, buckling the armoured flight deck lengthwise, blowing holes out the side of the hangar deck, and tearing a hole in the ship's bottom. *Taihō* sank an hour later. More than 600 men lost their lives. USS *Albacore* is shown here just before Operation *Forager* on 28 April 1944. (USNHHC)

**Above:** As well as *Taihō*, the carrier *Shōkaku* was attacked. The carrier was caught while in the process of refuelling and recovering its aircraft by the submarine USS *Cavalla*. Like Blanchard, Lieutenant Commander Kossler fired all six bow tubes at eight-second intervals. At least two of the torpedoes hit the carrier, one of which struck her starboard side forward and the other amidships, starting large fuel fires in the hangar bay.

The fires could not be brought fully under control and after about another hour of trying to save the carrier, Captain Hiroshi Matsubara issued the order to prepare to abandon ship. As his crew assembled on the flight deck, Matsubara tied himself to the ship. However, at 12.10 hours, with most of the crew still on deck, *Shōkaku* abruptly took on water forward and sank quickly bow-first, taking 1,272 men with her. Seemingly, Matsubara had not tie himself very tightly to his ship as he was washed overboard as it went down and he was forcibly rescued.[30] *Shōkaku* is seen here at Yokosuka on 23 August 1941, shortly after she was completed. (National Museum of the US Navy)

**Top right:** By the end of 19 June, Task Force 58 had survived the most concentrated attacks made against US carriers in the entire war. Remarkably, only two carriers, *Bunker Hill* and *Wasp*, and two battleships, *Indiana* (BB-58) and *South Dakota* (BB-57), suffered damage, but all remained fully operational. Thirty-one US aircraft were lost in the course of the day, of which seventeen Hellcats were lost in combat and four through other causes. Fourteen Hellcat pilots and thirteen other men were dead or missing. The Japanese had suffered shocking losses, with at least 220 carrier and forty land-based aircraft brought down. While further losses lay ahead for the Japanese, disaster would soon strike the US flyers as Mitscher took up pursuit of the Japanese fleet. Here a Japanese plane crashes during a night attack on TG 58.3 on 19 June, as seen from USS *Lexington*. (USNHHC)

**Bottom right:** A wounded pilot is helped from his cockpit having landed back on USS *Essex* during the fighting on 19 June. (USNHHC)

**Left:** Throughout the night, Mitscher continued to chase after the Japanese warships and the next day, 20 June, patrols were flown from the US carriers to try and locate the enemy fleet. Despite encountering a number of Japanese aircraft, it was almost 16.00 hours before what was believed to be a positive sighting of the enemy ships was established. It was calculated that Ozawa's force was 230 miles away, about maximum distance the strike aircraft could fly and still expect to get back to their carriers. But the main problem was that even an immediate launch would mean the aircraft returning in the dark, for which only a handful of pilots had training. But, with reserves of fuel becoming an increasing concern for Mitscher, he knew that he had to strike that day or see the Japanese escape. So, Mitscher gave his 'Launch em' order. 'Get the carriers', became the mantra of the aircrews preparing for the mission. In this photograph TBF Avenger torpedo bombers (centre background) and SB2C Helldiver dive bombers (foreground) are heading for the Japanese carriers on 20 June. (USNHHC)

**Below:** Mitscher's plan was to launch a 240-aircraft strike, but this was modified to 226. The launching from twelve carriers began at 16.24 hours. But, after the first wave had taken off it was discovered that the Japanese ships were, in reality, sixty miles further away, and Mitscher felt he could not take the risk of sending his aircraft such a distance at such a late hour, and the second wave was aborted. The Japanese fleet was located by the first wave as the sun was just beginning to set. Photographed by an aircraft from USS *Monterey*, here ships of the Japanese Carrier Division 3 are seen taking evasive action while under attack by American planes on 20 June. The ships present include an aircraft carrier, a heavy cruiser, and a battleship. (US Navy)

**Above:** As the Battle of the Philippine Sea unfolds, the Japanese aircraft carrier *Zuikaku*, in the centre surrounded by bomb bursts, and two destroyers are pictured here manoeuvring while under attack by US Navy carrier aircraft during the late afternoon of 20 June. *Zuikaku* was hit by several bombs during these attacks, though she skilfully avoided two torpedoes. The bombs started large fires which appeared to be out of control, but the crew fought the flames and the ship survived. (USNHHC)

**Top left:** Another view of Japanese Carrier Division 3 under attack in the late afternoon of 20 June. Ozawa knew the strike was coming, so his ships were in air defence formation, and he put every plane into the sky that he could, including fighter-bombers and dive-bombers, to try and protect his ships. The battleship in the lower centre is either *Haruna* or *Kongō*. The aircraft carrier *Chiyoda* is at the right. The photograph was taken from an aircraft operating from *Bunker Hill*. (USNHHC)

**Bottom left:** The Japanese carrier *Chiyoda*, seen here, suffered several near-misses during the air attacks on 20 June. Although the American airmen believed they had hit her more than once, she actually escaped relatively unscathed.

While four Japanese carriers had received some damage, only one, *Hiyō*, was sunk. The carrier was struck by two bombs, one of which detonated above the bridge and killed or wounded virtually everyone there. More seriously, the ship was struck by one torpedo dropped by a Grumman TBF Avenger from the light carrier USS *Belleau Wood*. The torpedo knocked out the starboard engine room and started fires but *Hiyō* was able to continue, albeit at reduced speed. Two hours later, a large explosion occurred when leaking fuel vapour ignited. The resulting fires could not be contained and *Hiyō* sank stern first shortly afterwards taking 247 men to their deaths. (National Museum of the US Navy)

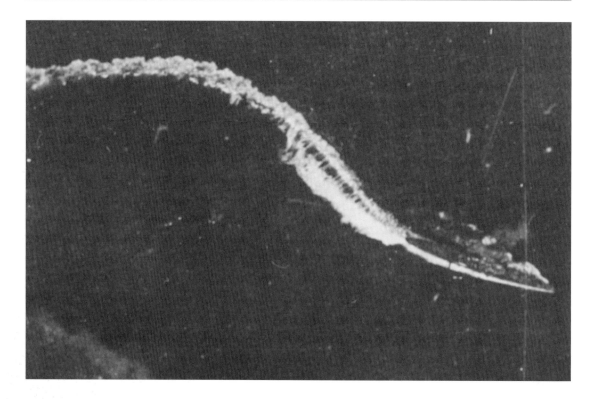

**Above:** A Japanese heavy cruiser is pictured taking evasive action while under attack on 20 June. (USNHHC)

**Right:** Lieutenant Ronald P. Rip Gift relaxes with other pilots in a ready room on board USS *Monterey* after landing following the strikes on the Japanese fleet late on 20 June. Note the instruction 'Get the Carriers' on chalkboard in the background.

Gift was one of the lucky ones. The American flyers had to navigate through the pitch black of the moonless Pacific night, but to help them Mitscher, risking being spotted by enemy submarines, ordered his carriers to turn on all their lights. Even so, eighteen aircraft crashed as they attempted their landings on the flight decks – many of the US Navy pilots had not received extensive training for night landings on carriers. Other pilots waiting for a chance to land back aboard their carrier were left circling until their fuel completely ran out, forcing them to ditch at sea. Nearby cruisers and destroyers typically serving as screens for the carriers quickly switched to rescue operations and managed to recover 143 of 185 of the airmen forced down into the ocean. Eighty aircraft were lost.

Chief Warrant Officer Cecil S. King Jr. was a witness to the events that night: 'That night, when they came back in, I was up topside, at my battle station. It was a memorable evening, because there were planes landing all over the place. It didn't matter what carrier they were from. The minute anybody flashed ready deck, somebody landed on it. Almost every landing was some kind of deck crash – They were running on fumes. There were planes going in the water everywhere … On the *Hornet* they passed the word to throw over anything that would float – wooden orange crates, anything. These guys out in the water – there were just people everywhere. It was an extremely dramatic occasion. I just couldn't believe what was happening.'[31] (USNHHC)

**Above:** Some of the crew of USS *Lexington* are pictured painting Japanese flags on the carrier's island to denote the 143 'kills' claimed by her Air Group 16. During the battle, and for the loss of 123 aircraft and 109 dead, the US Navy had destroyed nearly 600 enemy aircraft, sank two enemy fleet carriers, a light carrier, and two oilers, killing nearly 3,000 of the IJN's pilots and sailors.[32] The carrier fleet, Japan's most formidable weapon, had been irrevocably wrecked. Complete control of the vast expanse of the Pacific Ocean was finally in Allied hands and the operations against the Marianas could continue unhampered. (National Museum of the US Navy)

## Chapter 6

# BANZAI! – THE LAST BATTLE

## 7 July 1944

After three weeks of fighting on Saipan, two-thirds of the island were in American hands. Indeed, by the end of the first week of July 1944, the US forces on Saipan had squeezed Saitō's defenders into an area of Paradise Valley north of Tanapag. This, the last significant town held by the Japanese, was taken by the 27th Division, elements of which then pushed the Japanese back to Marpi Point at the island's northern extremity. There Saitō, sick, hungry and wounded, sheltered in a 'miserable' cave with the remnant of his command.

The drive towards Marpi Point had begun on 6 July. The 105th Infantry had been placed on the left flank of the 27th Division as it pushed up the left side of the island. On its right was the 165th Infantry, tasked with tackling the mountainous spine of Saipan. The 106th Infantry was in divisional reserve. Though moving through more favourable terrain, the 105th met spasmodic, though fierce resistance, and progress was slow, with the Japanese firing from well-hidden positions, which the Americans found hard to locate, and from a trench which cut across the Tanapag plain.

**Above:** A view taken from the beach near Tanapag, on Saipan's north-west coast, of part of the area in which the Banzai charge was made on 7 July. The attack was launched from the high ground in the distance, an area that was later termed Harakiri Gulch. (John Grehan Collection)

Disappointed by the rate of advance, at 07.00 hours on 6 July, the 105th Infantry and the left battalion of the 165th were ordered to advance and push their positions along the flat coastal plain as far as the village of Makunsha to bring them in line with the rest of the division.

Saitō was trapped, and when the Japanese had been in similar situations on Tarawa and the Marshall Islands, they threw themselves at their enemies in one final suicidal assault. That was just how they were to respond on Saipan.

On 6 July, Saitō issued his orders for a 'Banzai' charge to be made the following morning – one in which every man who could move, regardless of his physical state, would attack the Americans with whatever weapons were to hand. The latter, in the form of the 1st and 2nd battalions of the 105th Regiment, had been posted in a semi-circle on the Tanapag plain during the night of 6/7 July. Behind these units were the 105th's 3rd Battalion, and a short distance further back was positioned the artillery of the 3rd Battalion of the 10th Marines.

At 04.00 hours on 7 July, Saitō sent his bedraggled band to *Gyokusai* – die with honour. Shortly afterwards he committed suicide, as did Vice-Admiral Nagumo.

At 04.45 hours, just as daylight began to pierce the early morning sky, the sound of bugles echoed across the Tanapag plain. Moments later, a rag-tag army of thousands of Japanese soldiers, sailors, and, according to one witness, civilian construction workers, armed with rifles, spears, or just their bare hands, charged, yelling and screaming as they ran, or hobbled and limped towards the American lines. Swarming down the valleys and on to the narrow coastal plain, they found a gap between the 1st and 2nd battalions of the 105th Infantry and ran on towards the regimental headquarters. The Japanese may have been little more than a disorganized rabble, but Major Hoffman later recalled that, 'Here was a determination which was seldom – if ever – matched by fighting men of any other country'.[33]

'All hell broke loose,' remembered Lieutenant George O'Donnell of Company G of the 105th's 2nd Battalion, as the Americans were gradually forced back, in some cases into the streets of Tanapag itself. 'From our right and below us, there came thousands of Japs! For two hours they passed by, and came right at us. It was like a mob after a big football game, all trying to get out at once! We had a hard struggle keeping them from overrunning us, and had a field day, firing, firing until our ammunition started to run low. The closest any of them came was ten yards, and we were hitting them at four hundred and five hundred yards also.'[34]

The Japanese were slaughtered as they threw themselves at the 105th and the marine artillery, which fired at will over open sights at virtually point-blank range. The bodies of the attackers became piled so high in front of the guns, the marines had to move round them to retain an open field of fire – and still the Japanese kept coming. The infantry and marines hung on into the afternoon, despite heavy losses, when at last the 106th Regiment came to their help.

Among the relentless Japanese attackers was Mitsuharu Noda, Vice-Admiral Nagumo's yeoman who had been relieved of his duties now that his boss was dead. 'We were ordered there to be

**Left** At Marpi Point, Saitō, pictured here when he was commander of the First Air Fleet in 1941 or 1942, made the following statement as he ordered the remnants of his garrison to make one final charge against the Americans: 'Our comrades have fallen one after another. Despite the bitterness of defeat, we pledge, "Seven lives to repay our country" … Whether we attack or whether we stay where we are, there is only death. However, in death there is life. We must utilize this opportunity to exalt true Japanese manhood.' (USNHHC)

killed,' Noda once remarked. 'Some probably may have got drunk, just to overcome fear ... It was a kind of suicide ... We hardly had any arms. Some only had shovels, others had sticks. I had a pistol.

'I think I was shot at the second line of defence. Hit by two bullets in my stomach, one passing through, one lodging in me ... I woke up when [the Americans] kicked me and they took me to the field hospital.'

Noda was, unquestionably, one of the lucky ones, for the events that followed the *Gyokusai* were almost too horrible to witness. The plain was strewn with the bodies of the Japanese – 4,311 according to one source[35] – which were ploughed into mass graves by bulldozers. The 105th suffered almost 1,000 casualties.

**Above:** The battered shell of General Saito's and Vice-Admiral Nagumo's last command post at Marpi Point at the northern tip of Saipan. (John Grehan Collection)

**Right:** Japanese ships and various small craft on fire in Tanapag Harbor after being hit by Marine field artillery before the Banzai charge. Several larger ships, sunk earlier in the operation, lie offshore. (USNHHC)

**Below:** Another painting by the war artist Robert Benney, this is the scene that greeted the men of the 27th Division on the beach at Tanapag in the aftermath of Saitō's *Gyokusai* on 7 July 1944. (USNHHC)

**Right:** A dead Japanese soldier lies on the beach at Tanapag Harbor as several small Japanese ships still burn offshore after being hit by Marine artillery.

One of the positions that the Japanese almost overran was the regimental command post of the 105th, located about 800 yards south of Tanapag. 'There, however, they could not get through the defenses,' notes one account. 'The enemy spearhead was beginning to show the blunting accomplished by the desperate fighting of the units that had been overrun. At 1130, the depleted and tiring enemy was considered pretty well stopped, but fighting dragged on through the afternoon. By then, however, the impetus had entirely vanished from the attack, and some of the Japanese were turning grenades upon themselves.'[36] (USNHHC)

**Overleaf:** The bodies of dead Japanese soldiers litter a beach near Tanapag after the suicidal failure of their Banzai charge. This photograph was taken two days after the event by a combat photographer from the cruiser USS *Indianapolis*. (USNHHC)

**Left:** A number of the Medal of Honor awards that resulted from the fighting on Saipan were as a consequence of Saitō's *Gyokusai* on 7 July 1944. One of the posthumous recipients that day was Pfc Harold C. Agerholm, seen here, who was serving in the 4th Battalion, 10th Marines, 2nd Marine Division at the time. Noting his 'conspicuous gallantry and intrepidity at the risk of his life above and beyond the call of duty', the citation for the award goes on to state: 'When the enemy launched a fierce, determined counter-attack against our positions and overran a neighboring artillery battalion, Private First Class Agerholm immediately volunteered to assist in the efforts to check the hostile attack and evacuate our wounded.

'Locating and appropriating an abandoned ambulance jeep, he repeatedly made extremely perilous trips under heavy rifle and mortar fire and single-handedly loaded and evacuated approximately 45 casualties, working tirelessly and with utter disregard for his own safety during a gruelling period of more than 3 hours.

'Despite intense, persistent enemy fire, he ran out to aid two men whom he believed to be wounded Marines but was himself mortally wounded by a Japanese sniper while carrying out his hazardous mission. Private First Class Agerholm's brilliant initiative, great personal valor and self-sacrificing efforts in the face of almost certain death reflect the highest credit upon himself and the United States Naval Service.'

**Left:** Seen here in the centre with the cigarette in his mouth, Lieutenant Colonel William O'Brien, commander of the 1st Battalion, 105th Infantry Regiment, 27th Infantry Division, is in discussion with other officers on Saipan on 18 June 1944. O'Brien was killed during the Banzai attack on 7 July. For his actions that day he was another posthumous recipient of the Medal of Honor, the citation acknowledging that the award recognises a series of gallant actions, the first of which occurred on 20 June, two days after this picture was taken. (New York State Military History Museum)

 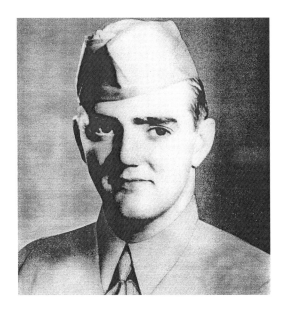

**Above left:** A portrait of Lieutenant Colonel William O'Brien. Of the events on 7 July, and O'Brien's part in them, his citation states the following: 'With bloody hand-to-hand fighting in progress everywhere, their forward positions were finally overrun by the sheer weight of the enemy numbers. With many casualties and ammunition running low, Lt. Col. O'Brien refused to leave the front lines.

'Striding up and down the lines, he fired at the enemy with a pistol in each hand and his presence there bolstered the spirits of the men, encouraged them in their fight, and sustained them in their heroic stand. Even after he was seriously wounded, Lt. Col. O'Brien refused to be evacuated and after his pistol ammunition was exhausted, he manned a .50-caliber machine gun, mounted on a jeep, and continued firing.

'When last seen alive he was standing upright firing into the Jap hordes that were enveloping him. Some time later his body was found surrounded by enemy he had killed.' (New York State Military History Museum)

**Above right:** That the 1st Battalion, 105th Infantry Regiment bore much of the brunt of the Japanese charge on 7 July is evidenced by the fact that another man in this unit, Private Thomas A. Baker, pictured here, was also a posthumous recipient of the Medal of Honor. His citation states:

'During the early stages of this attack, Sgt. Baker [the promotion was also posthumous] was severely wounded, but he insisted on remaining in the line and fired at the enemy at ranges sometimes as close as 5 yards until his ammunition ran out. Without ammunition and with his weapon battered to uselessness from hand-to-hand combat, he was carried about 50 yards to the rear by a comrade, who was then himself wounded. At this point Sgt. Baker refused to be moved any further stating that he preferred to be left to die rather than risk the lives of any more of his friends.

'A short time later, at his request, he was placed in a sitting position against a small tree. Another comrade, withdrawing, offered assistance. Sgt. Baker refused, insisting that he be left alone and be given a soldier's pistol with its remaining eight rounds of ammunition. When last seen alive, Sgt. Baker was propped against a tree, pistol in hand, calmly facing the foe. Later Sgt. Baker's body was found in the same position, gun empty, with 8 Japanese lying dead before him.' (US Army)

**Above:** A fourth posthumous Medal of Honor would be awarded as a result of the Banzai charge on 7 July, though in this case it would take the best part of six decades for the recipient, Captain Ben Salomon, to be duly honoured. As well as noting that he was yet another member of the 105th Infantry Regiment, what stood him out was the fact that he was a dentist, being the regimental dental officer of the 2nd Battalion.

Salomon was originally recommended for the Medal of Honor by Captain Edmund G. Love, the 27th Division's historian, but it was denied because he was considered ineligible by virtue of being a member of military medical personnel. It was not until 1 May 2002, more than a half-century following the end of the war, that this decision was overturned.

The citation states: 'Realizing the gravity of the situation, Captain Salomon ordered the wounded to make their way as best they could back to the regimental aid station, while he attempted to hold off the enemy until they were clear. Captain Salomon then grabbed a rifle from one of the wounded and rushed out of the tent. After four men were killed while manning a machine gun, Captain Salomon took control of it. When his body was later found, 98 dead enemy soldiers were piled in front of his position.' To date, he is the only dentist to receive the Medal of Honor.[37]

This picture, taken on 1 May 2002, shows President George W. Bush shaking the hand of Dr. Robert West after presenting him with the Medal of Honor on behalf of Captain Ben Salomon. (NARA)

**Right:** A Marine pictured soon after Saitō's *Gyokusai* on 7 July, as US forces move forward to reoccupy the ground that was temporarily lost to the charging Japanese. Entire reoccupation of the Marine positions was accomplished during the afternoon, and by 18.00 hours, almost all of the ground lost to the attackers was again in friendly hands. (National Museum of the US Navy)

**Right:** On the same day that the desperate fighting was taking place around Tanapag, Marines and tanks, such as this M4 Sherman photographed on 7 July, were 'mopping up' isolated pockets of enemy troops. (USNHHC)

**Above:** The burial of General Saitō on 13 July 1944. Before his suicide, Saitō delivered a farewell message that he wanted conveyed to all his soldiers in which he pledged to leave his bones on Saipan, 'as a bulwark of the Pacific'. The traditional Japanese method of suicide – *seppuku* – was for the individual to cut open his stomach. But this was a very slow and painful way to die. So, Saitō arranged for one of his officers to shoot him in the back of the head immediately after he had started cutting his stomach. (USMC Archives)

**Above:** One of the Japanese soldiers who survived the Banzai attack was Captain Sakae Ōba. In the immediate aftermath of the charge, Ōba and forty-six other men retreated into Saipan's rugged interior. By living off the land and raiding US camps for supplies, this small group of 'Hold Outs' remained at large in the jungles and coral caves on the island for 512 days, or about sixteen months. They were finally persuaded to surrender to US forces on 1 December 1945 – at which ceremony this picture was taken. (National Museum of the US Navy)

**Left:** In officially confirming his surrender, Captain Sakae Ōba presents his sword to Lieutenant Colonel Howard G. Kurgis USMC on 1 December 1945. On learning that he had survived the war, the Japanese authorities, who had presumed that Ōba had been killed in 1944, rescinded a 'posthumous' promotion to Major. (National Museum of the US Navy)

Chapter 7

# SUICIDE CLIFF

Though the Banzai charge had cost the lives of the majority of its participants, and their commander, Saitō, had taken his own life, there were still some Japanese soldiers left alive on the island, as well as many thousands of civilians, possibly as many as 4,000, crammed into the northern tip of Saipan.

While the attack had inflicted crippling losses on the 1st and 2nd battalions of the 105th Infantry, the rest of 27th Division was still able to resume its advance the following day, 8 July. But Holland Smith, astoundingly, saw the 27th Division as lacking drive and instead ordered the 2nd Marine Division to pass through the Army's ranks and take up the offensive to clear the enemy from those areas of the island they still occupied.

**Below:** Having been ordered by Holland Smith to eliminate any remaining Japanese resistance, the 6th Marines, with the 2nd Tank Battalion in support, duly fought its way forward. Here we see Marine Corps M4 Sherman tanks attacking Japanese positions in the village of Makunsha on 8 July. (USNHHC)

On the morning of the 9th, the American Marines and infantry attacked the last remnants of the enemy garrison. Easily dealing with scattered counter-attacks around Mount Marpi, which was bypassed in the last US advance, the airfield beyond was found to have been utterly devastated by bombardment.

By 16.15 hours, the Marines were at the coast, having advanced a total of 2,500 yards that day. The fire-scarred earth of Saipan lay behind. It was at this time that Vice-Admiral Turner duly declared the island secure. The next day an official flag-raising took place at Holland Smith's headquarters in Charan Kanoa. There was, however, one further tragedy to be played out on Saipan.

**Right:** In this photograph Marines are shown taking cover behind an M4 Sherman tank as they cautiously advance along a track while clearing Japanese forces from the northern end of the island of Saipan, 8 July 1944. (USMC Archives)

**Below:** One of a number of Japanese vehicles and assorted transport knocked out during bombing by US carrier aircraft near Tanapag. (National Museum of the US Navy)

**Left:** It was on 8 July that one of the Marine Corps tanks, that commanded by Sergeant Grant Frederick Timmerman (seen here) of the 2nd Battalion, 6th Marines, was advancing a few yards ahead of the infantry in support of an attack upon one of the Japanese positions.

'Sergeant Timmerman maintained steady fire from his antiaircraft sky mount machine gun until progress was impeded by a series of enemy trenches and pillboxes,' ran the wording of his citation for the Medal of Honor. 'Observing a target of opportunity, he immediately ordered the tank stopped and, mindful of the danger from the muzzle blast as he prepared to open fire with the 75mm, fearlessly stood up in the exposed turret and ordered the infantry to hit the deck. Quick to act as a grenade, hurled by the Japanese, was about to drop into the open turret hatch, Sergeant Timmerman unhesitatingly blocked the opening with his body holding the grenade against his chest and taking the brunt of the explosion.'

Although two members of the crew received slight wounds from the grenade, none were killed. All of the larger fragments were taken by Timmerman who knew the moment he stopped that grenade from dropping into the tank that he would die. (USNHHC)

**Below:** A Marine rests for a moment in a Japanese shrine during the operations on Saipan. (USMC Archives)

**Above:** An aerial view of Marines searching for enemy personnel or civilians who might be hiding in caves and brush-covered gullies near Marpi Point on 9 July 1944. (National Museum of the US Navy)

The civilians had been told that the Americans would torture and murder them, and rather than suffer such a terrible and ignoble fate, they preferred suicide. Some killed themselves secretly in the caves at Marpi Point, others threw themselves off the cliff there, in what one writer called 'a final orgy of death'. Whole families were seen throwing themselves to their deaths, arms linked. Even little children screamed 'Banzai' as they jumped off the 800-foot-high cliff.

An article written by Robert Sherrod was published in *Time* magazine which told the citizens of the United States the kind of war the Allies were fighting: 'You wouldn't believe it unless you saw it," said one marine. "Yesterday and the day before there were hundreds of Jap civilians – men, women and children – up here on this cliff [Marpi Point]. In the most routine way, they would jump off the cliff, or climbed down and wade into the sea. I saw a father throw his three children off, and then jump down himself. Those coral pockets down there under the cliff are full of Jap suicides.'

Another witness, Lieutenant Frederic Stott, saw a 'handful of soldiers, determined to prevent the surrender or escape of their kinfolks, who tossed grenades into the milling throng of men, women, and children, and then dived into the sea … The exploding grenades cut up the mob into patches of dead, dying and wounded, and for the first time we actually saw water that ran red with human blood.'[38] In was in this gruesome manner that the Battle for Saipan drew to a close.

**Left:** As we have seen, not all the Japanese were killed during the Banzai attack and there were still a number of them left alive on the island, and the slow process of driving the Japanese soldiers out of their subterranean hideouts continued. Here, a Marine can be seen throwing a grenade into an enemy-held cave. The total number of prisoners of war held on Saipan on 9 July stood at just 736, including 438 Koreans. But the post-campaign mopping up raised the total to 1,734 by 27 July, including 838 Koreans.[39] (USNHHC)

**Above:** A large Japanese flag captured by US forces on Saipan on 9 July is displayed for a photographer from USS *Indianapolis*. (National Museum of the US Navy)

**Above:** The mass suicides which took place on Saipan at the end of the American operation there, during which many individuals, soldiers and civilians alike, threw themselves to their death, took place at two main locations. One of these was at Marpi Point, the very northern tip of Saipan, at what today is known as Banzai Cliff. Note the memorials to the some of dead on the clifftop. (Courtesy of Jerrye and Roy Klotz)

**Below:** A US serviceman looks out over part of Banzai Cliff. Around 22,000 civilians were killed on Saipan, most being suicides. (USMC Archives)

**Above:** A short distance from Banzai Cliff, and slightly inland, is the equally chillingly named Suicide Cliff, which rises above Marpi Point Field. (via Historic Military Press)

**Below:** The flag raising ceremony held at Holland Smith's headquarters in Charan Kanoa on 10 July 1945. Admiral Spruance can be seen in the centre, whilst Holland Smith, with his holster visible, is on the right. (NARA)

**Right:** The work of rounding up remaining Japanese servicemen and civilians continues on Saipan. One of the Japanese who surrendered, Takeo Yamauchi, wrote of his experiences in one of the caves during those last days: 'The non-commissioned officer was a little dictator; he ordered the babies to be killed because they were making a noise that could give everyone away to the Americans. At this, one of the mothers got up and walked out of the cave. She said, "I'd rather die than kill my baby." But the mothers who were left did strangle their babies to death … the cave went quiet. All I could hear was the mothers crying. My only thought was of surrender. I told myself not to get involved in what was happening around me. But by the third day, the cave had started to stink, from the rotting bodies of the babies. I couldn't bear it anymore. That night of 14 July, I slipped quietly out of the cave. I had made up my mind to surrender.'[40] (USNHHC)

**Above:** A party of US Marines takes a break during the search for remaining Japanese servicemen and civilians still hiding in caves along Saipan's northern coastline near Marpi Point, 10 July 1944. (National Museum of the US Navy)

**Above:** Loudspeakers are used to try and persuade Japanese soldiers and civilians hiding in the caves near Marpi Point to surrender, 12 July 1944. Note the boats patrolling just offshore. (National Museum of the US Navy)

**Below:** Also pictured on 12 July 1944, a Japanese prisoner of war speaks via the loudspeakers at Marpi Point in an effort to convince his comrades to come out of hiding. (National Museum of the US Navy)

**Above:** Some of the civilians did seek help despite their fears of what the Americans might do to them. Many were in very poor condition, as Private First Class Tibor Torok witnessed: 'Some were carrying dead babies. The dead babies were covered with black, stinking flies. We had to bury the dead babies, but the women fiercely resisted this. They fought us, but we finally managed to bury them.'[41] One of the most moving images of the invasion of Saipan is this photograph of a Japanese family – a mother four children and a dog – who were found in a cave on Saipan by Corporal Angus Robertson on 21 June. (NARA)

**Above:** Guy Louis Gabaldon of the 2nd Marines, whom we read of earlier regarding the fighting in Garapan, achieved world-wide fame for persuading more than 1,300 Japanese soldiers and civilians to surrender rather than commit suicide. Gabaldon had lived from the age of twelve with a Japanese family and, naturally, had learned much of their language.

From his first night ashore, Gabaldon, operating beyond the front line on his own, had managed to persuade small numbers of Japanese to give themselves up. But it was on 8 July, the day after the Banzai charge, that he performed one of the most remarkable feats of the war. On the evening of 6 July, Gabaldon had set off on one of his nightly sorties but found himself cut off by the Japanese massing for the Banzai charge. He had to remain hidden until the next morning when he crept to the edge of the cliffs where he quickly captured two guards. After talking to the two men, he convinced one of them to return to the caves below. This was a tense time both for Gabaldon and the two Japanese.

However, shortly afterward a Japanese officer and some of his men walked slowly up from the caves and sat down in front of Gabaldon. Within an hour, hundreds of Japanese infantry, accompanied by civilians, began surrendering en-masse. He returned to his regiment with some 800 prisoners. He was recommended for the Medal of Honor, receiving instead the Silver Star. This, in turn, was upgraded to the Navy Cross in 1960.

Shown in this photograph by Sergeant John Fabian are two of the Japanese soldiers being taken prisoner. (USNHHC)

**Above:** Marines inspecting a destroyed Japanese H8K flying boat after the capture of Saipan. (National Museum of the US Navy)

**Right:** Photographed by Lieutenant Paul Dorsey, a party of Catholic nuns hear mass on Saipan for the first time after the fighting in 1944. Sister Maria Angelica Salaberria recalled the moment that her group was discovered by the advancing Americans: 'The place where the police had left us was a large clearing, with not a single tree for shelter. Furthermore, we were caught between Japanese and American crossfire. We spent the day lying face down on the ground, bullets whizzing continuously over our heads. A bomb fell close to Brother Oroquieta, but did not explode. At nightfall, a [US] soldier approached us to see if we were dead and was surprised to find we were alive.'[42] (National Museum of the US Navy)

**Top left:** Native Chamorros and Kanakas islanders help with repairing and building of roads in the aftermath of the Battle of Saipan. A census undertaken in 1937 indicates that the native islanders of Saipan included 3,143 Chamorros and 1,037 Kanakas. Nearly 3,000 of the islanders, mainly the Chamorros, were in an internment camp by the end of the battle. With most islanders sympathetic to the Allied cause, many, if not all, were soon released. (National Museum of the US Navy)

**Bottom left:** General Holland Smith visiting the 2nd Marine Corps Division Cemetery on Saipan in the summer 1944. (USMC Archives)

**Above:** Corporal James R. Martin USMC displays a sword he found amid the ruins of a Japanese officer's quarters during the fighting on Saipan in 1944. Engraving on the sword identified it as belonging to Captain Walter Nevins Flournoy USMC, who was taken prisoner by the Japanese on Guam in December 1941.

Flournoy survived his time in captivity. Remaining in the Marine Corps, he was awarded the Legion of Merit for his actions in the Korean War. The Japanese flag in the background is another trophy from Saipan. (National Museum of the US Navy)

**Above:** Altogether the Battle of Saipan cost the lives of 3,426 US servicemen, with a further 10,346 wounded. Here, a US sailor pays his respects to American servicemen who gave their lives in the fight for the island. (NARA)

**Right:** Lieutenant General Holland M. Smith, holding a M1 Carbine, makes a tour of men and installations at Saipan airport before leading the assault on Guam, the next objective of Operation *Forager*. (NARA)

**Left:** Located near the beach overlooking Tanapag Harbor, the American Memorial Park commemorates those Americans and Chamorro who died during the liberation of the Mariana Islands during the Second World War. Within the park is the Saipan American Memorial, which specifically honours the 24,000 American Marines and soldiers who died recapturing the islands of Saipan, Tinian and Guam during the period 15 June 1944 to 11 August 1944. (via Historic Military Press)

**Above:** Mirroring the scenes on Saipan, US Marines take cover during the initial landings on Guam on 21 July 1944. The largest island in the Marianas group, Guam had been an American territory before its occupation by the Japanese in December 1941. The fighting to liberate Guam, still part of Operation *Forager*, did not end until 10 August 1944. (USNHHC)

**Below:** The battle to capture the island of Tinian began three days after that on Guam, on 24 July 1944. Little could those Marines sent to wrest it from the Japanese that day, such as those seen here dismounting from an LVT, possibly have known that the island was destined to play a key role in the last, cataclysmic, acts of the Second World War. The Battle of Tinian concluded on 1 August 1944. (USNHHC)

Chapter 8

# 'HELL IS ON US'

The capture of the Marianas, and in particular the Japanese territory of Saipan, was, General Holland Smith declared, 'the decisive battle of the Pacific offensive. The capture of Saipan, he continued, had 'breached Japan's inner defense line, destroyed the main bastions, and opened the way to the home islands'.[43]

Mirroring his counterpart's thoughts, General Saitō had written that 'the fate of the Empire will be decided in this one action'. Vice-Admiral Shigeyoshi Miwa agreed, declaring that, 'Our war was lost with the loss of Saipan'.

**Above:** An aerial view of the first B-29 base on Saipan, Isely Field, after its construction following the capture of Saipan. The original temporary landing field on the site was built by the Japanese Navy in 1933. After its upgrade, following the attack on Pearl Harbor, it was renamed Aslito Field. In US service, the airfield was further renamed Isely Field in honour of Commander Robert Henry Isely, who was shot down and killed, by anti-aircraft fire, during an attack on Aslito Field on 13 June 1944. At the time, Isely's name was misspelt in official documents and reports as 'Isley', and it was by this incorrect spelling that the airfield was often originally referred. Today, the airfield serves as Saipan's international airport. (NARA)

**Above:** The runways of Saipan International Airport, formerly Isely Field, can be seen in the distance in this view taken looking south from the summit of Mount Tapochau. The image provides a sense of scale to the fighting that occurred on Saipan in June and July 1944. (Courtesy of Cla68)

**Top right:** Nicknamed *Joey*, this Republic P-47D Thunderbolt of the 19th Fighter Squadron, 318th Fighter Group, was pictured on Saipan in July 1944. (NARA)

**Bottom right:** As the original caption notes, 'an old Japanese strong point' was converted into the Base Operations centre for the B-29 units operating out of Isely Field. (NARA)

The loss of Saipan, being part of Japan's National Defence Zone, had major ramifications in Tokyo from a military perspective. So serious was the situation that it prompted Prime Minister Hideki Tojo to resign, for he could see that from the Marianas the US bombers would be able to reach Tokyo. 'When we lost Saipan,' remarked one of Hirohito's aides, 'Hell is on us'.

But it was the death of so many civilians, and particularly the mass suicides, which had the most profound effect on the Japanese people, for this was seen not as something fine and noble, but as an indication of desperation and failure. It was one thing to die fighting the enemy for the Emperor, but quite another to die for no reason. When Tojo resigned he was joined by his entire cabinet. The Chief of the Imperial Navy General Staff also stood down, and Emperor Hirohito, well aware that soon American bombers would be flying from the Marianas to strike the Japanese home islands, asked his Foreign Minister, Mamoru Shigemitsu, to find a diplomatic way to end the war, if possible.[44]

Tojo would be proven correct. Even before the Marianas had been fully secured, US Navy construction battalions began work upon a series of airfields on the islands, an effort which eventually saw the completion of one aerodrome on Saipan and two on both Guam and Tinian. Indeed, work on the first airfield for B-29s on Saipan started as early as 24 June 1944. It was exactly five months to the day when more than a hundred B-29s took off from Saipan for an attack on Tokyo – the first since the famous Doolittle Raid in 1942.

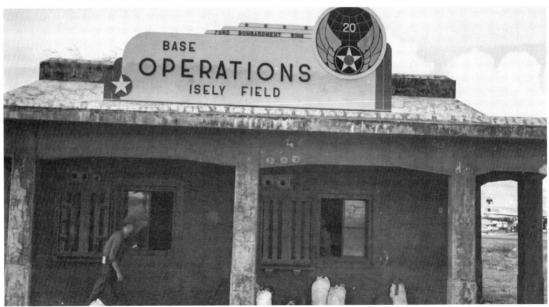

In the weeks and months that followed, the B-29s of the Twentieth Air Force ranged far and wide across the Japanese mainland. Over the course of the subsequent twelve months, the B-29s flew 29,000 missions, dropped 157,000 tons of explosives, which, by Japanese estimates, killed 260,000 people, left 9,200,000 homeless, and demolished or burned 2,210,000 homes.[45]

It is the missions of *Enola Gay* and *Bockscar*, however, for which the Mariana Islands-based B-29s are most widely known. It was their dropping of the atomic bombs on Hiroshima and Nagasaki which finally brought the Second World War to an end.

**Right:** A view of the activity on Isely Field in late 1944. Note the Boeing B-29 Superfortress that can be seen on the right. (NARA)

**Above:** It is said that the first B-29 to land at Saipan was that nicknamed *Joltin Josie: The Pacific Pioneer*. Flown by Brigadier General Haywood S. Hansell, the commander of XXI Bomber Command, and co-piloted by Major Jack J. Catton, of the 873rd Bombardment Squadron, it arrived at Isely Field on 12 October 1944. (NARA)

**Above:** Captain Ralph D. Steakley gives the crew of his Boeing B-29 their last-minute instructions before taking off from Saipan for the Japanese capital. They were, notes the original caption, 'the first over Tokyo from Saipan'. (NARA)

**Right:** Groundcrew load a wing tank on to a Lockheed P-38 Lightning, that nicknamed *Little Red Head*, at Isely Field in November 1944. (NARA)

**Below:** Boeing B-29 Superfortress *Tokyo Local* pictured taking off from Isely Field on Saipan en route to bomb targets in Japan. (NARA)

**Left:** A view of numerous B-29s in a crowded dispersal area on their airfield at Saipan, as seen through the Plexiglass nose of one of the bombers. (NARA)

**Above:** Armourers at Isely Field load a 500-pound incendiary bomb into the bomb bay of a B-29 Superfortress in preparation for a mission over Tokyo. The image was taken on 29 November 1944. (NARA)

**Overleaf:** Boeing B-29 *The Dragon Lady*, from the 871st Bombardment Squadron, 497th Bomb Group, pictured undergoing maintenance on Saipan. (US Air Force)

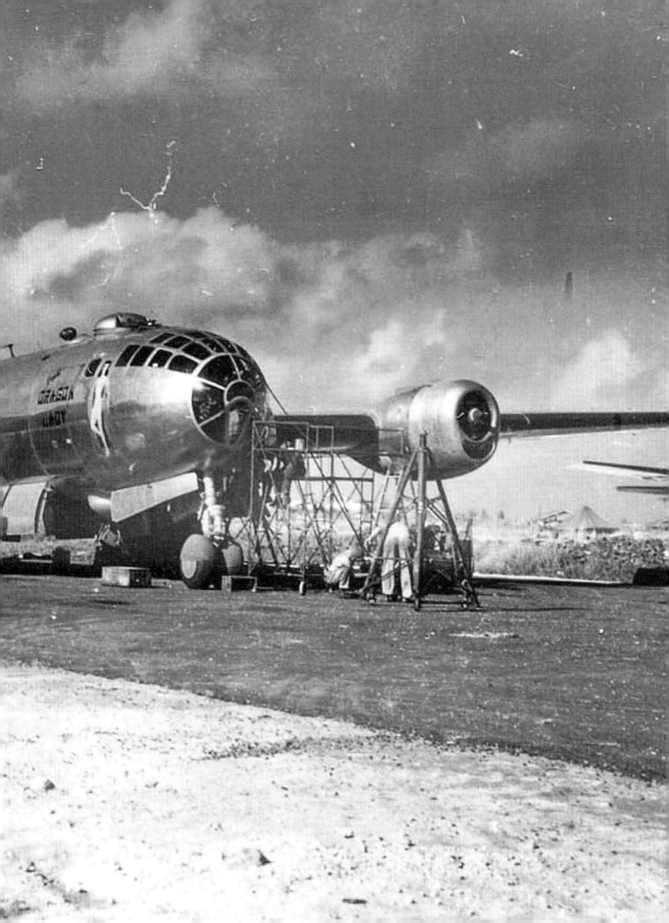

**Above:** A line of B-29s waiting to take-off from Saipan. The second of the bombers from the left, #42-24670 nicknamed *Ham's Eggs*, was damaged in a Japanese air attack on Saipan on 27 November 1944.
(NARA)

# NOTES AND REFERENCES

1. Francis Pike, *Hirohito's War, The Pacific War 1941-1945* (Bloomsbury, London, 2015), p.832.
2. Henry I. Shaw, Jr., Bernard C. Nalty, and Edwin T. Turnbladh, *History of U.S. Marine Corps Operations in World War II*, Volume 3 (US Marine Corps Headquarters, 1966), p.238.
3. ibid.
4. Adam Bisno, PhD, quoted from *Operation Forager: The Battle of Saipan* on .
5. Philip A. Crowl, *The War in the Pacific: Campaign in the Marianas* (Washington D.C., 1960), p.72.
6. ibid, p.78.
7. Quoted on the *TCPalm* website, www.eu.tcpalm.com.
8. Captain John C. Chapin, USMCR (Retd.), *Breaching the Marianas: The Battle for Saipan* (Marines in World War II Commemorative Series), p.1.
9. *The Japan Times*, 5 July 2014.
10. Major Carl W. Hoffman, *Saipan: The Beginning of the End* (Historical Branch, G-3 Division, Headquarters, U.S. Marine Corps, 1950), p.54.
11. Chapin, op. cit., p.2.
12. Henry, Nalty, and Turnbladh, op. cit., p.277.
13. James H. Hallas, *Saipan, The Battle That Doomed Japan in WWII* (Stackpole, Lanham, 2019), p.191.
14. Quoted in Victor Brooks, *Hell Is Upon Us, D-Day in the Pacific June-August 1944* (Da Capo, Cambridge MA, 2005), p.198.
15. ibid, p.207.
16. Robert Sherrod, *On to Westward: The Battles of Saipan and Iwo Jima* (Duell, Sloan and Pearce, New York, 1945), p.90.
17. Gordon L. Rottman, *Saipan & Tinian 1944: Piercing the Japanese Empire* (Osprey, Oxford, 2004), p.60.
18. Harold J. Goldberg, *D-Day in the Pacific, The Battle of Saipan* (Indian University Press, Indianapolis, 2007), p.131.
19. John Toland, *The Rising Sun, The Decline and Fall of the Japanese Empire 1936-1945* (Pen & Sword, Barnsley, 2011), pp.506-7.
20. Hoffman, op. cit., p.170.
21. Chapin, op. cit., pp.17-8.
22. ibid, p.18.
23. Narrative of Events, 2nd Battalion, 105th Infantry, 22 June to 3 July.
24. Brooks, op. cit., p.213.
25. Henry, Nalty, and Turnbladh, op. cit., p.333.
26. ibid.

27. Chester G. Hearn, *An Illustrated History: The U.S. Navy from 1775 to the 21st Century* (Zenith Press, St Paul, 2007), p.80.
28. Toland, op. cit., p.498.
29. Samuel J. Cox, Director NHHC, *H-032-1: Operation Forager and the Battle of the Philippine Sea*, June 2019.
30. ibid.
31. Quoted from 'One Big Turkey Shoot', *Naval History Magazine*, Vol.8, No.3, June 1994.
32. Samuel Eliot Morison, *History of United States Naval Operations in World War II: New Guinea and the Marianas, March 1944–August 1944, Vol. VIII.* (Little, Brown and Co., Boston, 1953), pp.152–3.
33. Commander David Moore USN (Retd.), *The Battle of Saipan - The Final Curtain*, .
34. Brooks, op. cit., pp.221-2.
35. Derrick Wright, *Pacific Victory, Tarawa to Okinawa 1943-1945* (Sutton, Stroud, 2005), p.90.
36. Henry, Nalty, and Turnbladh, op. cit., p.345.
37. For more information, please see: www.health.mil.
38. Goldberg, op. cit., p.201.
39. Henry, Nalty, and Turnbladh, op. cit., p.345.
40. Quoted in Jonathan Lewis and Ben Steele, *From Pearl Harbor to Hiroshima and Beyond, Hell in the Pacific* (Channel 4 Books, London, 2001), p.196.
41. Hallas, op. cit., p.275.
42. 'Battle of Saipan: A Missionary's Story', www.pirepoint.org.
43. General Holland M. Smith and Percy Finch, Coral and Brass, Fleet Marine Force Reference Publication 12-37, p.181.
44. Rottman, op. cit., p.88.
45. Richard Harwood, *A Close Encounter: The Marine Landing on Tinian* (Marines in World War II Commemorative Series), p.31.

# SELECT BIBLIOGRAPHY

Brooks, Victor, *Hell Is Upon Us, D-Day in the Pacific June-August 1944* (Da Capo, 2005)

Chapin, Captain John C., USMCR (Retd.), *Breaching the Marianas: The Battle for Saipan* (Marines in World War II Commemorative Series)

Crowl, Philip A., *The War in the Pacific: Campaign in the Marianas* (Washington D.C., 1960)

Goldberg, Harold J., *D-Day in the Pacific, The Battle of Saipan* (Indian University Press, 2007)

Hallas, James H., *Saipan, The Battle That Doomed Japan in WWII* (Stackpole, 2019)

Harwood, Richard, *A Close Encounter: The Marine Landing on Tinian* (Marines in World War II Commemorative Series)

Hearn, Chester G., *An Illustrated History: The U.S. Navy from 1775 to the 21st Century* (Zenith Press, 2007)

Hoffman, Major Carl W., *Saipan: The Beginning of the End* (Historical Branch, G-3 Division, Headquarters, U.S. Marine Corps, 1950)

Lewis, Jonathan and Steele, Ben, *From Pearl Harbor to Hiroshima and Beyond, Hell in the Pacific* (Channel 4 Books, 2001)

Morison, Samuel Eliot, *History of United States Naval Operations in World War II: New Guinea and the Marianas, March 1944–August 1944, Vol. VIII.* (Little, Brown and Co., 1953)

Petty, Bruce M., *Saipan: Oral Histories of the Pacific War* (McFarland & Co., 2009)

Pike, Francis, *Hirohito's War, The Pacific War 1941-1945* (Bloomsbury, 2015)

Rottman, Gordon L., *Saipan & Tinian 1944: Piercing the Japanese Empire* (Osprey, 2004)

Shaw, Henry I. Jr., Nalty, Bernard C., and Turnbladh, Edwin T., *History of U.S. Marine Corps Operations in World War II*, Volume 3 (US Marine Corps Headquarters, 1966)

Sherrod, Robert, *On to Westward: The Battles of Saipan and Iwo Jima* (Duell, Sloan and Pearce, 1945)

Sloan, Bill, *Their Backs Against the Sea: The Battle of Saipan and the Largest Banzai Attack of World War II* (Da Capo, 2017)

Symonds, Craig, *World War II at Sea: A Global History* (Oxford University Press, 2018)

Tillman, Barrett, *Clash of the Carriers: The True Story of the Marianas Turkey Shoot of World War II* (New American Library, 2006)

Toland, John, *The Rising Sun, The Decline and Fall of the Japanese Empire 1936-1945* (Pen & Sword, 2011)

Wright, Derrick, *Pacific Victory, Tarawa to Okinawa 1943-1945* (Sutton, 2005)

Y'Blood, William T., *Red Sun Setting: The Battle of the Philippine Sea* (Naval Institute Press, 2003)